# Social Services Federal Legislation vs. State Implementation

BILL BENTON
TRACEY FEILD
RHONA MILLAR

990-34

October 1978

## THE URBAN INSTITUTE
WASHINGTON, D.C.

The research forming the basis for this publication was funded by the U.S. Department of Health, Education and Welfare, Administration for Public Services, through Contracts No. SRS-500-75-0010 and No. HEW 105-78-2010.

The interpretations or conclusions are those of the authors and should not be attributed to the U.S. Department of Health, Education and Welfare, or to The Urban Institute, its trustees, or to other organizations that support its research.

ISBN 87766-237-1

UI 990-34


PLEASE REFER TO URI 23700 WHEN ORDERING

Available from:

Publications Office
The Urban Institute
2100 M Street, N.W.
Washington, D.C.  20037

List price:  $4.50

A/78/2M

TABLE OF CONTENTS

Page No.

Foreword . . . . . . . . . . . . . . . . . . . . . . . . . . . . . . . . . . . .  v

Acknowledgements . . . . . . . . . . . . . . . . . . . . . . . . . . . . . . .vii

I.   Introduction. . . . . . . . . . . . . . . . . . . . . . . . . . . . . .  1

     A.  Goals of Title XX . . . . . . . . . . . . . . . . . . . . . . . .  1
     B.  Scope of The Urban Institute Study. . . . . . . . . . . . . . .  4
     C.  Study Design. . . . . . . . . . . . . . . . . . . . . . . . . .  5
     D.  Overview. . . . . . . . . . . . . . . . . . . . . . . . . . . .  8

II.  Planning for Social Services. . . . . . . . . . . . . . . . . . . .  9

     A.  Participation and Influence . . . . . . . . . . . . . . . . . .  9
     B.  Coordination. . . . . . . . . . . . . . . . . . . . . . . . . . 23
     C.  Evaluation. . . . . . . . . . . . . . . . . . . . . . . . . . . 31
     D.  Needs Assessment in Social Services Planning. . . . . . . . . . 34
     E.  The State Budget and Title XX Planning Processes. . . . . . . . 39
     F.  Conclusion. . . . . . . . . . . . . . . . . . . . . . . . . . . 43

III. Financing Social Services . . . . . . . . . . . . . . . . . . . . . 47

     A.  Introduction. . . . . . . . . . . . . . . . . . . . . . . . . . 47
     B.  Cost Control. . . . . . . . . . . . . . . . . . . . . . . . . . 53
     C.  Lessons from P.L. 94-401. . . . . . . . . . . . . . . . . . . . 60
     D.  Conclusion. . . . . . . . . . . . . . . . . . . . . . . . . . . 64

IV.  Allocating Social Services Resources. . . . . . . . . . . . . . . . 69

     A.  Introduction. . . . . . . . . . . . . . . . . . . . . . . . . . 69
     B.  Changes in the Allocation of Resources Among Services . . . . 72
     C.  Changes in Allocation of Resources Among Client Groups. . . . 75
         1.  Effects on Women and Minorities . . . . . . . . . . . . . . 81
         2.  Effects on the Aging. . . . . . . . . . . . . . . . . . . . 92
     D.  Changes in Allocation of Resources Among Substate Areas . . .101
     E.  Purchase of Service . . . . . . . . . . . . . . . . . . . . . .109
     F.  Conclusion. . . . . . . . . . . . . . . . . . . . . . . . . . .113

V.  Organizing and Managing Social Services . . . . . . . . . . . . . .119

    A.  Introduction. . . . . . . . . . . . . . . . . . . . . . . . .119
    B.  Changes in Organizational Structure . . . . . . . . . . . . .122
    C.  Changes in Personnel. . . . . . . . . . . . . . . . . . . . .124
    D.  Training and Staff Development. . . . . . . . . . . . . . . .125
    E.  Statistics and Reporting. . . . . . . . . . . . . . . . . . .128
    F.  Net Effects on the Allocation of Worker Time. . . . . . . . .131
    G.  Conclusion. . . . . . . . . . . . . . . . . . . . . . . . . .133

VI.  Changing Roles and Responsibilities . . . . . . . . . . . . . . .139

    A.  Introduction. . . . . . . . . . . . . . . . . . . . . . . . .139
    B.  Effect of Title XX on Federal-State Working Relationships . .141
    C.  Federal Regional Office Support and Assistance. . . . . . . .142
    D.  Fiscal Accountability Requirements. . . . . . . . . . . . . .147
    E.  Extent of Preventive Measures to Limit Potential for
          Audit Exceptions or Federal Fiscal Sanctions. . . . . . . .150
    F.  Conclusion. . . . . . . . . . . . . . . . . . . . . . . . . .152

# FOREWORD

As is often the case with legislative reforms in the human resources area, the passage of the Title XX amendment to the Social Security Act was accompanied by much fanfare. Entirely new methods of planning and administering social services were contained in this legislation, and many people involved in the provision of services had great hope that significant programmatic changes would result from its enactment.

While many significant changes have occurred in the planning and administering of social services, the authors of this report suggest that there is little evidence that the results of these efforts have even begun to fulfill the original expectations. In a few cases, the changes that have resulted from the Title XX reforms appear to have gone in directions that are quite different from those implied in the original legislation.

In retrospect, such findings should probably not be all that surprising. The issues that were addressed by the Title XX legislation were among the most fundamental in public administration: accountability, public involvement, and the allocation of resources. Attempts at improving the management of social services in these areas face steep odds because the complexities involved in the administration of such services are enormous.

The authors of this report offer a number of recommendations regarding future roles and responsibilities for administering social services. It is hoped that these suggestions will provide those who are interested in improving social services with some effective methods for addressing some of the most pressing problems in this area.

Jeffrey J. Koshel, Director
Social Services Research Program

# ACKNOWLEDGEMENTS

The authors are appreciative of the assistance of the several HEW Project Officers who coordinated the activities of the Title XX project: Judith Hecht, Mary Jane Cronin, Andrew Solarz, Sylvia Vela, and Caryl Holiber. Valuable support and incisive review was also provided by Donna Lopatin and Howard White of the Administration on Aging.

Special thanks go to Jerry Turem, who provided overall direction to the project staff during the two years of the study. A number of other people who either are or were associated with The Urban Institute provided valuable assistance in the design and conduct of the research reported in this paper, including Sam Edwards, Suzanne Woolsey, Burton Dunlop, Tito de la Garza, Lydia Skloven, Chris Harrison, Joe Gueron, Malee Chow, George Corcoran, and Jessica Cannon.

The authors are grateful to literally thousands of people in 19 states who were interested enough in the future of social services in the United States to take the time to be interviewed, complete questionnaires, or assist us in gaining access to invaluable supporting material. We are particularly appreciative of the contribution of citizens of the eight states studied in-depth. The following people reviewed our work and coordinated our efforts in their jurisdictions:

   Bernd Schwarz, Arizona Department of Economic Security
   Benton Clark, California Department of Social Services
   Catherine Williams and Miriam Turnbull, Iowa Department
      of Social Services
   Myrna Goss and Reginald Carter, Michigan Department of
      Social Services
   Gregory Coler, New York Department of Social Services
   Sandy Brenneman and Ron Penny, North Carolina Department
      of Human Resources
   Chuck Bocci, Oregon Department of Human Resources
   Margaret Gregg, Texas Department of Human Resources

Hundreds of individuals across the country have reviewed and commented upon the 33 Title XX working papers which formed the basis for this document. Particularly important contributions on various drafts of this manuscript were made possible by the following persons:

Jerry Silverman, Office of the Assistant Secretary
for Program Planning and Evaluation, HEW
Candace Mueller, Director, Hecht Institute,
Child Welfare League of America
Peter O'Donnell, National Governors' Association
Beryl Radin, Associate Professor, Washington Public
Affairs Center, University of Southern California
Jack Hansan, Director of Governmental Affairs and
Social Policy, American Public Welfare Association

It is obvious, too, that neither state support nor a national perspective could have been obtained for this study without the contribution of the regional offices of HEW's Administration for Public Services. Coordinating regional efforts on the project's behalf were the following persons:

James Colarusso, Boston
Mel Herman, New York
Dick Sapanaro and Maurice Meyer, Philadelphia
Ed Schulz, Atlanta
Eli Lipshcultz, Chicago
Peggy Wildman and Ross Clinchy, Dallas
Bill Weisent and Ammi Kohn, Kansas City
Fred Lund and Ray Myrick, Denver
Jean LeMasurier and Lucy Ellison, San Francisco
Dick McConnell and Enid Welling, Seattle

Lastly, we would like to thank Alice Hill for providing special editorial services in the preparation of this paper. Rita Hogan did an outstanding job as Project Secretary for the study. The authors are grateful for their patience and diligence.

As in all reports of this nature, final responsibility for the analyses and interpretations rests with the authors.

# I. INTRODUCTION

Social services in the United States have, for the most part, evolved in the backwater of public policy. More than anything else, national service programs reflect the sincere but ad hoc concerns of the American people for the human needs of the poor, children, the unemployed, the aging, Native Americans, and disabled persons. Even today, social service policy is regarded as an incidental appendage of the public debate over national health insurance or welfare reform.

Nevertheless, the miscellany of national social service programs intimately touches the lives of millions of families and individuals in the form of day care for children, protective services for abused or neglected children and adults, family planning services, in-home and health-related services for the mentally and physically disabled, and family counseling. Information and referral services also function as the nerve center for virtually every other human service program.

Public debate leading to the first attempt at comprehensive social services legislation in the United States began in 1973. A wide diversity of interests (including representatives of the executive and legislative branches of the federal government, state social service agencies, the nation's governors, organized labor, and a host of other public, professional, philanthropic, and private organizations) labored with considerable intensity throughout 1973 and most of 1974. Out of these efforts emerged P.L. 93-647, the Social Security Amendments of 1974. Title XX of the Social Security Act was signed into law by President Ford on January 4, 1975.

## A. GOALS OF TITLE XX

Although there may be a considerable difference of opinion with regard to the intent of individual legislators and other major figures involved in the drafting and enactment of Title XX, it seems clear that the major goals of that legislation were:

1.  <u>To create a comprehensive national social services program.</u>

Even though separate social service programs (e.g., the Older Americans Act) were neither abolished nor merged with other programs to form Title XX, the Social Security Amendments of 1974 did represent the first attempt to establish a comprehensive national social services program. Service programs previously authorized under Titles IV-A and VI of the Social Security Act were consolidated in a new title which was separated, for the first time, from the titles authorizing the national income maintenance programs.

2.  <u>To redelegate authority for shaping social services programs to the states.</u>

Consistent with other legislation enacted as a part of the "New Federalism," P.L. 93-647 granted unprecedented authority to states to mold their own service programs toward the realization of five national goals:

> I.   Achieving or maintaining economic self-support to prevent, reduce, or eliminate dependency.
>
> II.  Achieving or maintaining self-sufficiency, including reduction or prevention of dependency.
>
> III. Preventing or remedying neglect, abuse, or exploitation of children and adults unable to protect their own interests, or preserving, rehabilitating, or reuniting families.
>
> IV.  Preventing or reducing inappropriate institutional care by providing for community-based care, home-based care, or other forms of less intensive care.
>
> V.   Securing referral or admission for institutional care when other forms of care are not appropriate, or providing services to individuals in institutions.

3.  <u>To focus federal attention on the end results of social services programs, rather than on the means by which services are provided.</u>

It was reasoned that, since so little was known about the efficacy of particular social services (means), it made little sense for the federal government to specify which service programs the states must provide to their citizens. It was further believed that, by granting states the flexibility to design unique service programs under Title XX, valuable experience would be gained from the resulting diversity of service programming which would more rapidly expand knowledge of service efficacy. Major responsibility for program evaluation was granted to the federal government.

4. <u>To make states accountable to their citizens, rather than to the federal government, for their social service programs.</u>

Title XX was not free of the procedural requirements generally associated with grant-in-aid programs. The most significant of the legislation's major new process requirements was that states must prepare a Comprehensive Annual Services Program (CASP) plan, open that plan to a period of public review and comment, and ultimately have the plan approved by the governor.

5. <u>To afford states an opportunity to make social services more universally available.</u>

Title XX contained several features which gave states the option to establish more universal social service programs. The minimum percentage of federal social services expenditures for categorically related (i.e., AFDC, SSI, Medicaid) recipients, for example, was reduced from 90 percent to 50 percent by Title XX. States were afforded the opportunity to provide services to individuals and families with incomes up to 115 percent of the state's median income. As a result, persons could be served under Title XX who were not tied in any traditional sense to public assistance programs. Title XX also authorized states to provide certain services (e.g., protective service and information and referral initially, and family planning later) to persons without regard to income. In addition, states were permitted to establish fee schedules (mandatory for most services provided to persons with incomes above 80 percent of the state's median income) to smooth the transition from free service for the poorest clients to, presumably, full-cost services for more affluent consumers.

It should be noted that a number of factors inhibited the realization of Title XX's goals. First, for many states, Title XX was not, in fact, a new program, since the ceiling on federal reimbursement for state social services remained at the $2.5 billion level that had been set in 1972. Second, the same federal and state bureaucracies that had administered Titles IV-A and VI were given the responsibility for administering Title XX. Third, the time available for any dramatic change, if, in fact, dramatic change was intended, was extremely short. States were required to publish their initial proposed CASP plans less than six months after Title XX was enacted. Had states waited for the promulgation of definitive regulations implementing Title XX, they would have had a mere three days to prepare and publish their CASP plans. Fourth, many of the key provisions of Title XX were optional--states were free to either accept or reject them. All these reasons contributed to speculation that state implementation of Title XX may not reflect the goals of the legislation.

B. SCOPE OF THE URBAN INSTITUTE STUDY

P.L. 93-647 required that HEW submit to Congress several reports on the implementation of Title XX: a special report on the appropriateness of the Federal Interagency Day Care Requirements (FIDCR), an annual report on the state social services programs funded by Title XX, and a special report on the implementation of the act itself, containing recommendations for change. To assist in the data collection and analysis necessary for both the annual and special implementation reports, HEW contracted with The Urban Institute to undertake an evaluation of the state implementation of Title XX.

The scope of that assessment was delimited in two major respects. First, it was a conscious decision that the Institute's evaluation not attempt to duplicate other examinations relevant to Title XX. For the most part, then, the Institute's evaluation of Title XX did not address issues pertaining to the appropriateness of the Federal Interagency Day Care Requirements (FIDCR), restate data available in HEW compilations of state CASP plans, or reformat data generated under the Social Services Reporting Requirements (SSRR) system set in place by Title XX regulations. Second, the Institute's examination did not address a central issue relevant to Title XX's implementation: its effect on the consumers of social services. It was felt that so little was known about the efficacy of social services prior to Title XX that it would be virtually impossible to detect any client effects, let alone those attributable to state implementation of P.L. 93-647.

The Institute's study of Title XX contrasted the legislation's intended effects with its actual effects in each of the following major areas:

- o The processes of planning and social services priority-setting.

- o Financing the nation's social services.

- o The allocation of social services resources.

- o The organization and management of state social service agencies.

- o The roles and responsibilities of major organizations involved in the administration of social services.

## C.   STUDY DESIGN

The Urban Institute study design involved the following four components:

1. Analysis of service allocation data

Data on costs, clients, and services were developed for five states for
the periods prior and subsequent to the implementation of Title XX.

2. Personal interviews

Over 600 structured interviews of key individuals involved with Title XX
at the state and local level were conducted by Institute staff in eight states.

3. Mail-out questionnaires

Questionnaires were completed by senior state officials, administrators of
provider agencies, and service workers in 19 states as a part of a cooperative
effort with HEW and the National Institute for Advanced Studies.

4. Regional office instruments

For each of the 51 jurisdictions (50 states and the District of Columbia)
administering Title XX, the regional offices of HEW's Administration for Public
Services completed an Institute-prepared instrument dealing with topics similar
to those covered in the personal interviews.

The participation of individual states in each of the four components of
the study design is shown in table 1. The states examined were selected because
of their willingness to participate and their diversity of experiences (i.e.,
ceiling vs. non-ceiling, state vs. locally administered programs, and "umbrella"
vs. single-purpose social service agencies).

In spite of the project scale, hard data about the implementation of a
program as new as Title XX were, in many instances, not available. Even where
data were available, extrapolation of state-specific observations to the
national experience was not always appropriate. What was available was a wide
variety of perspectives (e.g., intergovernmental, private, public, consumer,
and provider) concerning the implementation of Title XX in several states.
Nevertheless, the qualitative and quantitative data gathered, in spite of their

## TABLE 1

## State Participation in The Urban Institute Title XX Study

STUDY COMPONENTS

| Participating States: | Quantitative Cost Client & Service Data | Personal Interviews | Mail-Out Questionnaires | Regional Office Instruments |
|---|---|---|---|---|
| Arizona | | X | X | X |
| California | | X | X | X |
| Colorado | | | X | X |
| Connecticut | | | X | X |
| Florida | | | X | X |
| Georgia | | | X | X |
| Iowa | X | X | X | X |
| Louisiana | | | X | X |
| Massachusetts | | | X | X |
| Michigan | X | X | X | X |
| Missouri | | | X | X |
| New York | X | X | X | X |
| North Carolina | X | X | | X |
| Oregon | X | X | X | X |
| Pennsylvania | | | X | X |
| Texas | | X | X | X |
| Virginia | | | X | X |
| Washington | | | X | X |
| Wisconsin | | | X | X |
| Wyoming | | | X | X |
| Remaining 31 Jurisdictions | | | | X |

limitations, should contribute to a more informed discussion of the effects of Title XX even where a definitive answer to a particular question cannot be provided.

D.  OVERVIEW

The analyses that follow are designed to provide persons who have some understanding of and interest in social services and public policy with additional insight into what has actually happened since January 4, 1975. Specifically, these analyses are intended to identify the ways in which state implementation of a major piece of federal legislation appears to have produced results other than those contemplated by the individuals, agencies, and organizations instrumental in its passage.  In several respects, the analyses are inconclusive, since Title XX procedures and policies are still relatively young and dynamic.

Title XX is now at a crossroads.  During the next few years, actions will be taken (or not taken) that will determine the legislation's ultimate contribution to national social services policy.  Whether Title XX will emerge as the centerpiece of the nation's social services program or become simply another source of federal funds remains an open question.

## II.  PLANNING FOR SOCIAL SERVICES

A major goal of the Title XX legislation was to establish a uniform and comprehensive process of planning for social services.  The typical state plan for social services prior to Title XX was an arcanum, its existence known to many, its contents known to few.  There was no federal mandate that the plan be bound, distributed, subject to public review, or approved by the governor.  The pre-Title XX state plan for social services was, in fact, a plan only in the loosest sense.  Its relevant portions were essentially an evolving laundry list of services a state could provide to its eligible citizenry.

Major goals of the Title XX initiative included increased public participation, improved coordination among human resources planning systems, increased use of evaluation data and other criteria of program effectiveness in establishing program priorities, and a closer relationship between resource allocations and service needs.  The extent to which these objectives have been achieved has depended largely upon the relationship (or lack thereof) between the budget and CASP planning processes in each state.

### A.  PARTICIPATION AND INFLUENCE

A key purpose of the Title XX planning process was to provide an opportunity for citizen participation.  This objective was to be met by requiring that each state's Comprehensive Annual Services Program (CASP) plan be subject to public review before it could take effect.  HEW's regulations implementing Title XX stipulated:

> A State's services plan does not become effective until the public review process is completed in accordance with sections 222.23, 228.34, and 228.35.

> The purpose of the public review process is to enable the residents of each State to participate meaningfully in the State decision making processes with respect to the States services plan. The public review process is intended to assure that each State has provided opportunity for prior public participation of Title XX clients, Title XX advisory groups, public and private organizations, public officials, and the general public in needs assessment, identification of priorities and allocation of resources throughout the development of the plan.

Title XX's public review requirement was designed to do more than simply assure that the public would have an opportunity to participate in social services decision-making. It also represented one of the legislation's fundamental assumptions--that citizen participation would serve as a means of accountability. It was further assumed that this accountability to the public would substitute for the accountability of states to the federal government which characterized the legislation that preceded Title XX (Titles IV-A and VI) of the Social Security Act.

1. Extent of Participation

The data collected by The Urban Institute's regional office survey generally indicate that the perceived degree of public involvement in the social services planning process was greater by the end of the second year of Title XX's implementation than it had been during the period prior to Title XX's enactment. In only three states was the degree of public participation perceived to have declined since the implementation of Title XX. In seven other states, the extent of participation was seen as unchanged. The experience of these seven states may be particularly interesting, because in each instance participation was perceived to have increased during the first year, only to fall back to its pre-Title XX level during the second year.

Although the overall level of participation in social services priority-setting has remained above its pre-Title XX levels, in nearly all of the eight states studied closely by the Institute, public participation has declined sharply since the first year of implementation. The following factors appear to be primarily responsible for this decline:

a. <u>Several states have recently reached their ceiling (i.e., maximum use of federal fund allocation) on Title XX expenditures</u>. Rather than use a zero-base approach and make new resource allocation decisions each year, states appear reluctant to reconsider the decisions they made only a year earlier. In one jurisdiction at ceiling, state officials generally tried to discourage public participation in social services planning because Title XX did not provide any new money. Nevertheless, where service programs are being threatened or cut back, public participation may again be stimulated.

b. <u>Planning for social services in most states is constrained by the state budgetary process</u>. It is not unusual for the major decisions affecting social services priority-setting to be made, months <u>before</u> a proposed CASP plan is issued, as a part of the state budgetary process. It may be expected that, to the extent they are aware that major decisions are resolved in budget rather than the CASP process, members of the public will participate in the more meaningful of the two processes.

c. <u>To some extent, the novelty of Title XX has worn off</u>. Two years ago the implementation of Title XX was the primary focus of activity for social services professionals. Discussion of various aspects of Title XX highlighted conferences at the national, regional, and local levels. In addition, great effort was expended simply to find out what Title XX meant and what its practical implications were.

It is the shared perspective of senior state administrators and administrators of agencies providing social services under contract to state social services agencies that a dual dynamic is at work. As suggested by the data presented in table 2, it appears that state agencies have attempted, and are perceived by those outside the state agency as having been successful, to both encourage public participation and continue the service program which had existed prior to Title XX.

2. Participants in Title XX Decision-making

The only mandatory state action to stimulate public involvement in Title XX decision-making is the provision of a 45-day period for review and comment. States are encouraged, however, to go beyond the mandatory provisions of Title XX and its regulations to meaningfully involve persons outside the state social service agency in social services decision-making. To assess the effectiveness of steps taken by the states to open up the Title XX planning process, respondents in the eight-state in-depth study and observers in the HEW regional offices were asked the following question:

> Based on your experience with the state, how would you
> rate the level at which various individuals, agencies
> and organizations participated and influenced decisions
> on Title XX?

A summary of these data appear in table 3, and are discussed below.

a. Social Services Department Leadership. Prior to Title XX, the state agency's leadership was seen as being "head and shoulders" above other actors, the closest rival being the SSD's own regional office staff. Although the SSD has not lost its preeminent position in social services priority setting, and is not expected to do so within the next three years, there has been a substantial growth in the number of organizations which are at least moderately active and influential in the process. Nevertheless, it is the SSD which retains ultimate control over social services decisions, and the following elements of the Title XX regulations support this conclusion:

TABLE 2

Comparison of Current Goals of Title XX
Planning with Actual Result

|  | "Opens Up" the Social Services Planning Process[a] | | Continues Existing Social Services Program[a] | |
|---|---|---|---|---|
|  | Yes | No | Yes | No |
| Senior State Administrator Perceptions of Goal for Title XX Planning | 81.3 (148) | 18.7 (34) | 80.9 (144) | 19.1 (34) |
| Administrator of Provider Agency Perceptions of Actual Result of Title XX Planning[b] | 65.6 (82) | 34.4 (43) | 92.2 (106) | 7.8 (9) |

Source:  The Urban Institute Title XX Study: Senior Social Services
Administrator Survey.
a.  Percentages are shown rounded to one decimal.  Absolute number of
responses appears in parentheses.
b.  Excludes respondents indicating "don't know."

TABLE 3

Participation and Influence of Individuals, Organizations,
and Groups in Social Services Decision-Making

| | Extent of Participation and Influence | | | |
|---|---|---|---|---|
| Organization or Group | Pre-Title XX | First Year | Second Year | Within 3 Years |
| SSD Leadership[a] | 4.2 | 4.2 | 4.2 | 4.2 |
| Umbrella Agency | n.a. | n.a. | 3.8 | 4.0 |
| Services Division(s) | n.a. | n.a. | 3.7 | 3.9 |
| Governor's Office | 2.4 | 3.1 | 3.0 | 3.2 |
| Legislature (incl. Staff) | 2.6 | 3.0 | 2.8 | 3.5 |
| State Budget Office/OMB | 2.5 | 3.1 | 3.0 | 3.3 |
| State Agency on Aging | 1.9 | 2.7 | 2.6 | 3.2 |
| Area Agency on Aging | 1.5 | 2.3 | 2.4 | 2.9 |
| Other State Agencies | 2.5 | 3.1 | 3.0 | 3.4 |
| Mental Health | n.a. | n.a. | 2.5 | 2.9 |
| CETA | n.a. | n.a. | 1.7 | 2.2 |
| SSD Regional Office Staff | 3.0 | 3.3 | 3.0 | 3.5 |
| Local Service Agency/Office | 2.4 | 3.1 | 2.8 | 3.3 |
| Local Government | 1.9 | 2.5 | 2.3 | 2.9 |
| Service Providers | 2.6 | 3.1 | 3.2 | 3.4 |
| Client Groups | 1.8 | 2.7 | 3.0 | 3.1 |
| Other Groups | 2.4 | 3.4 | 1.9 | 3.9 |
| Average Assessment | 2.4 | 3.0 | 2.9 | 3.4 |

---

Source:  Regional Office Instruments and In-Depth Interviews.
Note:    Scale is from 1 (denoting little or no participation and influence)
to 5 (indicating extensive participation and influence).
a.  SSD refers to state social services department regardless of title.
"n.a." denotes separate data not collected for these periods.

o <u>Single state agency</u>. Each state is required to designate an "appropriate state agency" to administer Title XX. In addition to the fact that the predecessor programs to Title XX were also administered by social service departments, the characteristics which an appropriate state agency must possess (most notably, rulemaking authority) virtually dictate that Title XX be administered by social service departments.

o <u>Public review as input</u>. The public review and comment provisions of Title XX are mechanisms for obtaining <u>input</u> by individuals, organizations, and groups outside the SSD into decisions made by the state agency. Nothing in the Title XX law or regulations requires an SSD to act on that advice.

o <u>Gubernatorial sign-off</u>. One of the mechanisms of public account- ability afforded by Title XX is gubernatorial sign-off on the proposed and final CASP plans. Among the eight states surveyed in the Institute's in-depth study, gubernatorial sign-off has either been delegated back to the social services agency or become a perfunctory task.

b. <u>Governor's Office</u>. After a substantial increase in participation and influence during the first year of Title XX's implementation, the level of activity of governors and their offices in social services decision-making appears to have leveled off, according to the data presented in table 3. This pattern is not expected to change substantially within the next three years. In spite of the role of governors in securing the passage of Title XX, several factors exist that account for their declining interest in the administration of that program:

o <u>Governors tend to be more concerned with resolving specific issues than in the day-to-day management of affairs of state</u>. The effect of the ceiling on Title XX has often been to lock-in existing programs. To the extent that no issues are generated (e.g., reduction in programs), the involvement of governors is unlikely.

o <u>Title XX does not satisfy governors as having functioned as the comprehensive social service legislation they had envisioned</u>. Title XX was originally supported by governors who viewed it as a broad redelegation to states of the responsibility for structuring their own social service programs, free of the constraints associated with more categorical sources of funds. Restrictions in the Title XX regulations and the federal ceiling have limited the ability of governors to use Title XX as the vehicle for comprehensive social services planning.

o <u>In many respects gubernatorial involvement in Title XX is a "no win" proposition</u>. If the only decisions the governor can make with regard to social services are unpleasant ones, there is little incentive for a progressive governor to get involved in Title XX. Even in the best of times, social services are seldom the kind of programs that elected officials want to administer since they are often redistributive (i.e., they involve reallocating resources from one segment of the population to another). Governors, through the National Governors' Association, have supported an increase in federal social services expenditures.

c. <u>Legislators and Their Staffs</u>. One category of participants in social services decision-making whose activity and influence are expected to increase over the next three years is state legislatures. At the end of the first year of Title XX implementation, three factors were cited as contributing to the rise in legislative involvement in Title XX decision-making.

o <u>Involvement in the state budgetary process</u>. As will be discussed in greater detail, the state budget process acts as at least a moderate constraint on CASP planning in 43 of the 51 jurisdictions administering Title XX. Further, as the state budget process is increasingly recognized by interested parties as setting the framework for the CASP, state legislators are increasingly the focus of attention and pressure from groups particularly affected by Title XX (i.e., service providers and advocates).

o <u>Growth of legislative staff</u>. In each of the eight states examined in the Institute's in-depth study, state legislators and their staffs were observed to be increasingly involved in matters previously handled exclusively within the executive branch of state government. One mechanism for legislative involvement is budget "language" (i.e., written statements of legislative intent included in appropriations measures). Other mechanisms of legislative involvement, in addition to regular hearings and visitations, include legislative audits and reviews and the formation of special committees to deal with issues related to Title XX.

d. <u>State Budget Offices</u>. The executive agency most involved with social services priority setting, other than the SSD itself, is frequently the state budget office. An increasingly important aspect of state budget office involvement is the funding of multiple social service programs. In several instances, state budget offices have initiated intertitle transfers (i.e., the moving of service programs into and out of Title XX).

e. <u>State and Area Agencies on Aging</u>. Both state and area agencies on aging have become more active and influential in social services decision-making. The directors of state and area agencies are often able to assume roles that the heads of social services components of Title XX agencies cannot. The directors of state agencies on aging frequently deal with the heads of the Title XX agencies as peers, which may not be the case of service programs administered by an umbrella agency. Area agencies, too, are frequently more closely linked to local governments (especially councils of government) than are the local departments of social services or the local social services offices in state-administered programs.

Increasingly, however, it appears that state and area agencies on aging are the pursued rather than the pursuer. Funding of programs for the aging, particularly through Title VII (Nutrition) of the Older Americans Act, has increased significantly over the past few years, while Title XX reimbursement has not expanded for states at ceiling. Joint funding of services that were previously funded exclusively by Title XX has occurred, or has been proposed, in each of the eight states studied in-depth.

f. <u>Other State Human Resource Agencies</u>. The activity and influence of state agencies, other than those discussed above, in social services priority setting and implementation have also increased substantially since the inception of Title XX. Agencies most frequently cited in this regard are health, corrections, juvenile and youth services, education, vocational rehabilitation, child welfare (where separate from the Title XX agency), development disabilities, and mental health agencies. Little involvement was reported on the part of Comprehensive Employment and Training Act (CETA) personnel or administrators.

g. <u>SSD Regional Office Staffs</u>. The roles of the regional or district offices of the state social services agencies in the implementation of Title XX vary considerably among the eight states examined in the Institute's study. In two jurisdictions the district or regional office staffs were abolished for reasons apparently unrelated to Title XX (e.g., a concern about excessive overhead costs). In those states where regional or district offices of the SSD are well-staffed, they generally appear to have played a growing role in the planning and administration of social services programs since the implementation of Title XX. This development appears to have been stimulated by the opportunity afforded by Title XX for substate planning and state decisions to decentralize such Title XX-related activities as purchase of service contracting.

h. <u>Local Service Agency Offices and Staffs</u>. The local departments of social services agencies and their staffs have played a moderate role in Title XX priority-setting. Their level of activity and influence has been, and is expected to continue to be consistently lower than that of regional SSD offices.

One particularly interesting facet of local office participation in Title XX has been the participation of public agency employees. During the first year of Title XX implementation, service workers often voiced strong concern about paperwork, confidentiality, and other aspects of Title XX's eligibility and reporting process. During the second year of the title's implementation, the level of visible frustration among service workers appears to have subsided.

i. <u>Local Governments</u>. At the end of the first year, the participation of local governments in social services decision-making (particularly in states with locally administered social services programs) was substantially greater than the level that was perceived to exist prior to Title XX's implementation. The involvement of local governments, in the opinion of participants and observers, appears to have declined during the second year. In several instances local governments expressed their concern that they are not being permitted by the SSD to assume an effective role in social services priority-setting.

Even in states whose social services programs are nominally county-administered, local discretion may be sharply limited by the existence of state-mandated services and the ceiling on federal social service expenditures. These two factors combine to force jurisdictions to apply virtually all of their Title XX resources to the mandated services. The flexibility granted local governments under these circumstances is often merely the freedom to generate additional revenue (from local or other sources) to sustain optional (i.e., nonmandated) services.

In addition to their roles in priority-setting, local governments are often providers of social services under contract to the SSD or local Title XX agency. In a few cases, local governments have borne the major responsibilities for substate planning and needs assessment.

j. <u>Service Providers</u>. The activity and influence of service providers appear to be substantially increased under Title XX, a trend that is expected by observers to continue. The providers most frequently cited as being involved in the Title XX process were vendors of day care, mental health, homemaker/chore, family planning, and child welfare services, as well as services to the developmentally disabled, the aging, and the mentally retarded. Not infrequently, these providers have formed coalitions to strengthen their leverage on the Title XX agency on matters of service allocation, purchase of service procedures, and audit policy. Provider agencies were also called upon to participate in needs assessment activities and to provide testimony in support of state agency budget requests.

As the data presented in table 4 suggest, provider agencies have tended to be more active in the Title XX process than the social service workers themselves. Considerable concern was expressed by respondents in one state, for example, that providers were dominating the planning process.

k. <u>Client Groups</u>. Representatives of service consumer interests have generally been less active and influential in social services decision-making than the representatives of provider interests. Consumer participation has, however, increased substantially since the implementation of Title XX. Among the most frequently mentioned client groups involved in

TABLE 4

Involvement of Local Agency Social Service Workers
and Provider Agencies in Development of
Most Recent CASP Plan

| Nature of Activity | Percent "Yes" | | Percent "No" | |
| --- | --- | --- | --- | --- |
| | Social Service Workers | Provider Agencies | Social Service Workers | Provider Agencies |
| Attended Public Hearing | 17.4 | 66.9 | 82.6 | 33.1 |
| Presented Testimony (Oral Presentation) at Public Hearing | 10.5 | 39.7 | 89.5 | 60.3 |
| Reviewed CASP Plan | 26.9 | 68.6 | 73.1 | 31.4 |
| Submitted Written Comments on CASP Plan | 15.8 | 39.5 | 84.2 | 60.5 |
| Served on Statewide Planning Committee, Task Force, or Working Group | 10.4 | 20.4 | 89.6 | 79.6 |
| Served on Regional, District, or Local Planning Committee, Task Force, or Working Group | 14.4 | 31.8 | 85.6 | 68.2 |
| Participated in Needs Assessment | 25.5 | 45.7 | 74.5 | 54.3 |
| Other Significant Actions | 5.9 | 28.6 | 94.1 | 71.4 |

Source:  The Urban Institute Title XX Study: Senior Social Services
Administrator Survey.

social services priority-setting during the second year of Title XX were the aging, the mentally retarded, the handicapped, consumers of day care services, migrants, the blind, the deaf, community action agencies, and welfare rights organizations.

Instead of participation by rank-and-file consumers, however, client involvement has often been on the part of organized representatives and articulate advocates of provider interests ("captive clients"). This lack of rank-and-file consumer participation in social services decision-making is not very surprising when one considers the media generally afforded for participation in Title XX decision-making. These media include public hearings, display advertisements, opportunity for CASP plan review and submission of formal comments, involvement in advisory committees and task forces, and opportunities for testimony as part of the state (or local) budget process. These are media that tend to favor articulate and organized interests. Efforts to secure more representative consumer interests have included client and general population surveys, often as a part of state or local needs assessments.

1. Other Groups. The experience of other groups (i.e., individuals, organizations, and agencies in addition to those discussed thus far) is particularly interesting. The activity and influence of these groups was observed to have risen significantly during the first year of Title XX and to have declined during the second, and is expected to rise dramatically during the next three years. Although this category of respondents included a wide variety of actors, the most frequently mentioned other participants were the federal regional offices (year 1) and Title XX advisory groups and provider coalitions (year 2).

B.  COORDINATION

A key feature of planning under Title XX, in contrast to its predecessors, was to be the coordination of social services priority-setting programming with that of other human resources programs.  States, for example, are required to include in their CASP plans a statement of

> how the planning and the provision of services under
> the program will be coordinated with and utilize
> the following programs:
>
> (1)   Under the Social Security Act:
> (i)    title IV-A, AFDC (including WIN);
> (ii)   title IV-B, Child Welfare Services;
> (iii) title XVI, SSI; and
> (iv)  title XIX, Medical Assistance (Medicaid); and
> (2)   Other appropriate programs for the provision of
> related human services within the state--for example,
> programs for the aging, children, developmentally
> disabled, alcohol and drug abusers; programs in
> corrections, public education, vocational rehabili-
> tation, mental health, housing, medical and public
> health, employment and manpower.

1.  Limiting Factors

There appear to be two major factors which have limited the role of Title XX as the national vehicle for coordinated social services.

a.  Contrary to popular opinion, Title XX does not mandate coordination.  What is mandated is a description of what coordination may or may not take place.  Permissible levels of prospective coordination may range from none to extensive.  Further, there is no mandatory description of what coordination has actually taken place during the prior planning period.  Finally, since the descriptions included in CASP plans are often cast only in the most general terms, determining whether states have deviated from the coordination objectives contemplated in their CASP plans becomes difficult, if not impossible.

b.  There are many disincentives to coordination.  Not only is there no viable penalty for non-coordination, there are powerful disincentives to coordination with other human resources programs at the state and local levels. State CASP plans may include human services not funded through Title XX. However, these other services must be operated under the same regulations that govern services funded through Title XX. That is, other services have to comply with contracting, reporting, eligibility, and CASP plan amendment requirements. Further, publication of other HEW-funded programs in the CASP plans, for example, does not relieve the state or local agency of the responsibility to publish separate plans for those other programs. A recent HEW study (Ties That Bind) observed that HEW "requires every state receiving funds under its 46 formula grant programs to submit or annually update 24 separate state plans and eight separate applications or agreements."

2. Extent of Coordination

Table 5 indicates the extent of coordination (here defined as SSD actions to involve others in social services decision-making) under Title XX. These data indicate that, from the perspective of the HEW Regional Offices, the level of coordination across the country has declined somewhat from that perceived to exist during the first year of Title XX's implementation. Nevertheless, the extent of participation still is perceived to be higher than the level which existed prior to Title XX. It is notable, too, that the overall assessment of the degree of coordination is expected to increase within the next three years.

A summary of the major coordinative mechanisms in the eight states examined in the Institute's study is presented in table 6. Also presented are the special steps taken by Title XX agencies to involve persons or groups that might not otherwise be involved in Title XX planning.

3. Efficacy of Coordinative Mechanisms

In addition to simply describing the nature of coordination in each jurisdiction, respondents in the eight states studied were also asked to

TABLE 5

Extent of Coordination in 50 States and the
District of Columbia

| Organization or Group | Level of Coordination | | | |
|---|---|---|---|---|
| | Pre-Title XX | 1st Year | 2nd Year | Within 3 Years |
| Governor's Office | 1.6 | 2.0 | 1.9 | 2.3 |
| Legislature (incl. staff) | 1.6 | 2.0 | 1.7 | 2.2 |
| State Budget Office/OMB | n.a. | n.a. | 1.9 | 2.3 |
| State Agency on Aging | 1.6 | 2.2 | 2.0 | 2.4 |
| Area Agency on Aging | 1.4 | 1.8 | 1.8 | 2.3 |
| Mental Health | n.a. | n.a. | 2.0 | 2.2 |
| Vocational Rehabilitation | 1.7 | 2.0 | n.a. | n.a. |
| CETA (Manpower Planning Councils) | 1.4 | 1.6. | n.a. | n.a. |
| Other State Agencies | 1.7 | 2.2 | 2.2 | 2.6 |
| Client Groups | 1.6 | 2.2 | 2.0 | 2.3 |
| Local Governments | 1.6 | 2.1 | 1.7 | 2.2 |
| SSD Regional Office Staff | 2.1 | 2.5 | 2.3 | 2.8 |
| Local Social Service Staff | 1.8 | 2.1 | 2.1 | 2.6 |
| Other | 2.0 | 2.9 | 2.2 | 2.5 |
| Average Assessment | 1.7 | 2.2 | 2.0 | 2.4 |

Source:  Regional Office Instruments
Note:    1 denotes minimal effort in coordination; 2 denotes active solicitation
of input only; 3 denotes fully coordinated planning; and n.a. indicates that
data were not accumulated.

TABLE 6

Coordinative Mechanisms in Selected States

| State | Coordinative Mechanism | Steps to Involve Special Groups |
|---|---|---|
| Arizona | ° Advisory Committee<br>° Contracts w/COGs<br>° Regional Hearings | ° Contract w/Navajo Nation<br>° HEW-Sponsored Indian Capacity Building |
| California | ° Advisory Committee<br>° Interagency Agreements<br>° Governor's Office of Planning and Research | ° Display Ads in Foreign Language Press<br>° County Initiatives |
| Iowa | ° Interagency Task Force<br>° State and District Advisory Committees<br>° Interagency Agreements<br>° ICF/MR Initiative | ° Consumer Representation on Advisory Committees<br>° Rural Hearings |
| Michigan | ° Advisory Council<br>° Interagency Agreements<br>° Public Hearings | ° Wayne County (Detroit) Needs Assessment of Low-Income Persons |
| New York | ° State Advisory Committee<br>° District Advisory Committees<br>° "De-separation" of Income Maintenance and Services | ° Contract w/Aging<br>° Consumer Representation on Advisory Committees<br>° Display Ads in Foreign Language Press |
| North Carolina | ° Interagency Planning Committee<br>° State Advisory Committee<br>° Citizens' Committee on Title XX | ° Waiting Room Survey (Wake Co.)<br>° NCSU Needs Assessment<br>° General Population Survey |
| Oregon | ° Interagency Agreement<br>° Informal Mechanisms | ° County-Based Needs Assessment |
| Texas | ° State and Regional Advisory Council<br>° Regional Meetings<br>° Interagency Agreement<br>° Title XX Newsletter | ° Location of Hearings |

assess the efficacy of a variety of coordinative mechanisms. Their responses appear in table 7 and are discussed below.

a. Advisory Committees, Task Forces, etc. Although advisory committees are not required by Title XX, nearly every state established an advisory committee, task force, or similar body at the state and/or sub-state level.

State experience with advisory committees has been mixed. In the eight states studied closely, some advisory bodies established the first year have become defunct, others have been reconstituted in an effort to revitalize them, and others have been subordinated to pre-existing advisory groups.

In spite of their limitations, advisory committees were seen as one of the more effective mechanisms of coordination.

b. Public Hearings. A second frequently utilized coordinative technique under Title XX has been public hearings, public meetings, and the like. Widely used the first year, public hearings were less frequently held the second year and, if held, were generally less well attended in the eight states studied. Reasons for this decline included bad experiences the first year, less promotion, and a general feeling that the major decisions in Title XX were made by the end of the first year. Respondents often remarked that public hearings seldom provided an environment conducive to the resolution of substantive issues.

Although general Title XX public hearings played a smaller role during the second year, special issue meetings (e.g., those organized to prevent budget cutbacks or to affect the use of P.L. 94-401 funds) were well attended.

TABLE 7

Efficacy of Coordinative Mechanisms

| Coordinative Mechanisms | Average Assessment |
|---|---|
| Advisory Committee, Task Forces, etc. | 3.3 |
| Public Hearings | 2.8 |
| Display Advertisements | 2.3 |
| Workshops & Training Sessions | 3.1 |
| Formal Agreements (E.g., Aging) | 3.0 |
| Joint Funding | 3.0 |
| Other (Interagency Staffing, Written Comments & Open Administrative Meetings) | 3.7 |

Source:  The Urban Institute Title XX Study: 8 State In-Depth Study.
a.  Responses to the question "How would you assess the efficacy of the following as coordinative mechanisms in this state?" were scaled from 1 (denoting worthless) to 5 (denoting invaluable).

c. <u>Display Advertisements</u>. It is somewhat ironic that the coordinative mechanism felt by respondents to be the least valuable is the only one mandated by federal Title XX regulations. There is no evidence, in the sample states at least, that the display advertisements brought Title XX into the consciousness of significant numbers of persons who might otherwise have been unaware of social services. One state respondent, for example, suggested that the display advertisement yielded "one public comment for $50,000 . . . hardly a productive investment."

d. <u>Workshops and Training Sessions</u>. One coordinative mechanism respondents viewed as at least moderately valuable is workshops and training sessions. Where the information-sharing is the objective, a small group setting which affords opportunity for participant interaction may be more appropriate than a larger or more formal meeting. Workshops or training sessions may be particularly appropriate for providing information on purchase of service policy, program reporting requirements, or service outcome evaluation models.

e. <u>Formal Agreements</u>. A clear message received from respondents was that formal cooperative agreements are not self-implementing. In most of the eight states examined closely, cooperative agreements between the state Title XX agency and the state agency on aging had been negotiated. With few exceptions, these agreements contained rather broad provisions that periodic meetings and general coordination would take place. In few instances, however, had even these general provisions been implemented.

Rather than the <u>beginning</u> of a coordinative process, these agreements were often seen by the signatories as the <u>end</u>. For the most part, too, the initiator of the cooperative agreement was not the Title XX agency but the state agency on aging.

f. <u>Joint Funding</u>. One of the most promising instruments of coordination is joint funding of service programs. Modest examples of this mechanism abound. It is not unusual for Title VII of the Older Americans Act, for example, to fund the noon nutritional component of a Title XX-funded senior citizens center. The school lunch program is being used to defray the costs of Title XX day care for children. Increasingly, too, CETA staff are used as personnel in human services agencies.

Nevertheless, the obstacles to joint-funding are substantial. In addition to variations in each program's coordination, reporting, and accounting requirements, each program has different rules concerning the type of work that is allowable and which fees, if any, can, must, and cannot be collected. One "horror story" of the trials associated with joint-funding was related by an area agency on aging. The director of the area agency was extremely proud of the agency's creative use of Title XX, Community Services (OEO), Older Americans Act, and CETA funds to support a program to winterize the homes of the elderly. After considerable calculation, the area agency must tell the client something like the following: "You <u>can't</u> (CETA) pay for the carpentry involved, you <u>must</u> (Title XX) pay a fee for the weather-stripping, and you <u>may</u> (Older Americans Act) make a voluntary contribution for the insulation."

g. <u>Other Mechanisms</u>. A wide variety of coordinative mechanisms, in addition to those identified above, were reported by respondents as being of more than moderate utility. Examples included the exchange of staff between agencies and the outstationing of service staff in Social Security Administration offices.

C.   EVALUATION

Under Title XX, evaluation of program effectiveness is both a federal and state responsibility. The legislation states that "the Secretary (of HEW) shall provide for the continuing evaluation of State programs for the provision of services" and that "the Secretary shall make available to the States assistance with respect to the content of their services program, and their services program planning, reporting, administration and evaluation."

Although states are not required to evaluate their social services programs, they are required to include in their CASP plans a statement of the "purpose, scope of timing of current and proposed evaluations, and the schedule for dissemination of evaluation reports."

At the end of the first year's evaluation of the implementation of Title XX, the Institute observed that, "the increase reported in the degree of utilization of evaluation data was generally less than that reported for any of the other dimensions surveyed . . . In some respects this can, perhaps, be attributed to the long lead time required to produce the results of credible evaluation of program effectiveness." Nevertheless, most respondents indicated their intent to utilize program evaluation data to a greater extent in the future.

In the opinion of the regional offices, the degree of utilization of evaluation data did not change for slightly more than half the jurisdictions (27 of 51) during the past year. This may reflect the general dearth of evaluative data.

This impression is supported by a recent survey of state evaluation activities performed under contract to HEW. That study examined the extent to which state social services agencies had undertaken program evaluation studies. In all, 6 states were identified as high performers (i.e., with 6 to 18 studies completed or in progress), 18 states were identified as medium performers (i.e., with 1 to 3 studies), and the remaining 27 states were identified as low performers (i.e., with no studies completed or in progress). These data indicate that more than half the jurisdictions administering Title XX across the country have neither completed nor undertaken a single study of the effectiveness of the programs they administer. Nevertheless, the predominant perception among regional office respondents was that the use of evaluation data would increase over the next three years. In fact, no respondent predicted a decline (see table 8).

This optimism is generally shared by the respondents in each of the eight states examined in the Institute's study. This shared perception, however, may reflect three diverse dynamics:

o  In states with little or no evaluation activity, there is a feeling that, in effect, there is nowhere to go but up. A danger in this belief, however, is that responsible officals may assume that things will improve automatically and will, therefore, fail to undertake necessary initiatives at the state level to bring about the desired improvement.

o  In several states the evaluation and monitoring efforts have recently been expanded, and it is anticipated that data from such initiatives will be increasingly utilized in social services planning. Although laudable, a potential pitfall of this assumption is that the data produced will not be utilized in the decision-making process.

o  Finally, several states have existing competencies in program evaluation. The challenge in these states is to increase the degree to which data from these efforts are utilized in social services priority-setting.

TABLE 8

Anticipated Degree of Use of Evaluation Data
over the Next Three Years

| | Number of Jurisdictions | | |
| --- | --- | --- | --- |
| | Absolute Frequency | Relative Frequency (Percent) | Adjusted Frequency (Percent) |
| Much Less Than Second Year | 0 | 0.0 | 0.0 |
| Less Than Second Year | 0 | 0.0 | 0.0 |
| No Change | 8 | 15.7 | 19.5 |
| More Than Second Year | 25 | 49.0 | 61.0 |
| Much More Than Second Year | 8 | 15.7 | 19.5 |
| No Response | 10 | 19.6 | -- |
| Total | 51 | 100.0 | 100.00 |

Source:  Regional Office Instruments

The perspective offered by one respondent at the end of the first year's evaluation seems as appropriate today as it did a year ago.

> The future of social services evaluation [is] a "chicken and egg" situation. On the one hand decision-makers may be reluctant to rely on less than adequate evaluations. On the other hand good evaluations may not be undertaken unless decision-makers have the interest (i.e., provide the resources), patience, and foresight which are part of the environment needed to produce good evaluations.

D.  NEEDS ASSESSMENT IN SOCIAL SERVICES PLANNING

The federal mandate for states to conduct needs assessments is one of the strongest requirements in the Title XX regulations. Each state's CASP plan is required to

> describe the steps taken to assure that the needs of all residents of, and all geographic areas in, the State are taken into account in the development of the services plan. The description shall include the data sources used (or to be used).

During the first year of Title XX, as determined from a review of FY 1976 CASP plans, all but three of the 51 jurisdictions administering Title XX undertook some form of needs assessment. Most frequently, due to time constraints during the first year, such efforts were restricted to the use of pre-existing data, limited surveys or studies, or polling the membership of the Title XX committee or task force and providers of social services (see table 9).

Two trends emerge when the second-year experience in needs assessment is compared to that of the first year. First, states with a 21-month planning period undertook no new needs assessment. Second, those states that did undertake a second needs assessment effort tended to rely more on provider and client or citizen questionnaires than on program or census data.

TABLE 9

Needs Assessment Methods Used by States for
Comprehensive Annual Social Services
Planning under Title XX

| Method | Number of States Using Method | | % of All Methods Used | |
|---|---|---|---|---|
| | FY1976 | FY1977 | FY1976 | FY1977 |
| Program or Census Data | 31 | 27 | 34 | 29 |
| Survey or Study | 23 | 22 | 26 | 24 |
| Provider Questionnaire | 12 | 18 | 13 | 20 |
| Citizen or Client Questionnaire | 8 | 13 | 9 | 14 |
| Provider or State Agency Plans/ Proposals | 7 | 6 | 8 | 7 |
| Social or Economic Indicators | 7 | 3 | 8 | 3 |
| Information & Referral Lists | 2 | 3 | 2 | 3 |
| Total | 90 | 92 | 100% | 100% |

Source:  U.S. Department of Health, Education and Welfare, Administration for Public Services, Office of Human Development compilations from state Title XX Comprehensive Annual Services Program plans.

Note:   A state may use more than one type of method.

In FY 1976, 48 of the 51 jurisdictions (the 50 states and the District of Columbia) reported their needs assessment activities; 3 states indicated no needs assessment was conducted.  In FY 1977, 11 states reported that no new needs assessments were conducted, and 3 states did not report.

Perhaps as critical as the quality of the data is the extent to which the data are actually used in the process of resource allocation. From the perspective of senior state administrators, the use of needs assessment data in setting social service priorities can best be described as moderate (see tables 10 and 11). In the opinion of regional office respondents, needs assessments were the principal determinants of social services priorities in only four states. The primary use of needs assessment data to date has been to provide a basis for improved needs assessment in the future.

The extent to which the results of these future needs assessments will actually be used remains an open question. There are different criteria of utility for assessment of cross-progammatic needs than for assessment of the need for a single service or the needs of a particular population. First, comprehensive social services planning requires that a comparison of the relative needs of various populations for the entire range of services be made. Second, in order to be useful for optimizing the allocation of resources, needs assessment data must be analyzed in conjunction with program effectiveness evaluation data. The latter data presume that the objectives of social services programs have been specified in measurable terms. This has seldom been the case in social services, where the five national Title XX goals (while providing a general framework for analysis) are rarely operationalized by the states. Third, it is not sufficient to merely assess demand (needs) without a simultaneous assessment of the existing supply. Few states have adequate and comparable data on the level of services currently being provided by both public and private agencies.

There are a number of other factors which may also limit the use of needs data in the setting of social services priorities. One of the most critical

TABLE 10

Senior State Social Service Administrators'
Perceptions of the Use of State and Local
Needs Assessments in Title XX Planning

| | Responses | | | | Percent Distribution of Yes Responses |
| | Yes | | No | | |
| | # | % | # | % | |
|---|---|---|---|---|---|
| Provided a basis for improved needs assessment process in future | 112 | 84 | 22 | 16 | 34 |
| Selective use of needs assessment data in social services priority setting | 88 | 67 | 43 | 33 | 27 |
| Use for minimal compliance with federal Title XX requirements | 78 | 61 | 50 | 39 | 24 |
| Served as the major determinant in social services priority setting | 48 | 34 | 92 | 66 | 15 |
| Total | | | | | 100% |

---

Source: The Urban Institute Title XX Study: Senior Social Services Administrator Survey.

TABLE 11

Extent to Which State Agency Needs Assessments
Were Utilized in Determining Priorities for
Social Services

| | Number of Jurisdictions | | |
| --- | --- | --- | --- |
| | Absolute Frequency | Relative Frequency (Percent) | Adjusted Frequency (Percent) |
| Little or No Use | 4 | 7.8 | 9.3 |
| Less than Moderate Use | 9 | 17.7 | 20.9 |
| Moderate Use | 14 | 27.5 | 32.6 |
| More than Moderate Use | 10 | 19.6 | 23.3 |
| Principal Determinant | 4 | 7.8 | 9.3 |
| No Needs Assessment | 2 | 3.9 | 4.6 |
| No Response | 8 | 15.7 | -- |
| Total | 51 | 100.0 | 100.0 |

Source:   The Urban Institute Title XX Study of HEW Regional Office Survey.

elements in effectively using needs assessment is the timing of that
activity in relation to the decision-making process.  In the state
Title XX programs studied in-depth, the use of needs assessment findings
was often limited by the fact that, although the raw data were available
at the time planning decisions were made, the analysis of the data was
not.  Unanalyzed data are not particularly useful to policy makers in
making program choices.

Even when needs assessments are timed to meet the Title XX planning
schedule, their final impact can be limited by the lack of integration
between the state and local budget processes and the CASP planning cycle.

E.    THE STATE BUDGET AND TITLE XX PLANNING PROCESSES

During the second year of Title XX implementation it has become
increasingly obvious to observers and participants that the controlling
factor in state decision-making concerning the Comprehensive Annual
Services Program plan is very often the state budget (see table 12).

In 43 of the 51 jurisdictions administering Title XX it is believed
that the state budget acts as at least a moderate constraint on CASP
decision-making.  In 13 states that state budget is seen as controlling
Title XX decision-making completely.

This growing awareness has manifested itself in a sharp decline
in public participation in some states and, perhaps worse, a sense of
frustration among persons who were active in the Title XX planning process,
but who discovered that the critical decisions were being made elsewhere.
If the budget process continues to control CASP decision-making, it seems
likely that the CASP process will become a rote exercise and that the very
public whose increased participation was desired by Title XX will, quite
literally, be "a day late and a dollar short."

TABLE 12

State Budget as a Constraint on CASP Decisions

| Extent of Constraint | Number of States | |
| --- | --- | --- |
| | Absolute Frequency | Relative Frequency |
| None | 4 | 7.8 |
| Minimal | 4 | 7.8 |
| Moderate | 16 | 31.4 |
| Major | 14 | 27.5 |
| Complete | 13 | 25.5 |
| Total | 51 | 100.0% |

Several suggestions were made to improve the linkages between the CASP planning and state budget cycles:

1. Change the format of state budgets and CASP plans to permit a comparison between the two.

Even where the state budget does not completely control CASP plan options, the two documents are closely related. Nevertheless, in most instances it is difficult, if not impossible, for anyone outside the state social service agency to compare the two.

Another change that would seem particularly appropriate in CASP plans would be the inclusion of at least the prior year's expenditure and service data so that the current year's CASP plan may be viewed (as are budgets) in a multi-year context. Another way in which a comparison could be achieved would be by changing the format of state budgets. Legislatures may, however, be quite comfortable with line-item budgets, making comparison of those costs to specific Title XX service programs very difficult. Such modification, however, may be one means of enabling legislative leadership to play a more meaningful role in Title XX decision-making.

2. <u>Permit states to formulate a multi-year CASP plan</u>.

Respondents in each regional office were asked to indicate the optimal length of the CASP program period for each state if one's objective were to more closely coordinate the Title XX planning and state budgeting processes. These data are summarized in table 13.

TABLE 13

Preferred Length of Program Period

| Number of Months | Number of States | |
| --- | --- | --- |
| | Absolute Frequency | Relative Frequency |
| 12 | 29 | 56.9 |
| 24 | 16 | 31.4 |
| 36 | 4 | 7.8 |
| No Response | 2 | 3.9 |
| Total | 51 | 100.0% |

It would appear that a biennial CASP plan, concurrent with a biennial budget, would permit closer integration of the two documents. In states with an annual budget process, however, recommendations to move to a multi-year CASP plan may simply be prompted by desire to make a rote process less onerous by making it less frequent. There are some tradeoffs, too, in that the longer the period covered by the CASP plan, the more probable will be the need to undertake a plan amendment. These considerations may be reflected in the fact that a three-year plan was suggested for only four states, and no regional office respondent suggested a CASP program period longer than 36 months.

3.    Permit full integration of the Title XX and budget processes.

The 1976 amendments to general revenue sharing, in order to promote public participation in the allocation of those funds, permit the integration of the public hearing and budget process provided the latter safeguards the opportunity for public attendance and participation.

A similar provision in Title XX could not only enhance coordination between the budgetary and planning processes, but enhance meaningful public participation as well.

4.    Exercise the flexibility currently afforded to adjust the planning and budget cycles.

States are afforded substantial flexibility as to when they publish their proposed CASP plans (i.e., any time more than 90 days prior to the beginning of a program year) and when their final CASPs must be published (i.e., any time after a 45-day period of public review and comment and before the beginning of the program period).

In designing the CASP/budget linkage it seems that CASP timing should depend primarily on the timing of periods of critical decision-making.  For example, if the critical decision-making period takes place within the state social services agency prior to the submission of its proposals to the governor or legislature, the proposed CASP may be appropriately issued before those departmental recommendations are made so that public review and comment can take place.

It would appear that by exercising existing flexibility and more liberal and constructive use of federal waivers, the budget and planning processes for social services can be more closely linked in most states.

F.   CONCLUSION

   1.   CASP planning is not comprehensive, and in many key respects the
CASP is not a plan at all.

   Although a substantial improvement over the state plans of the pre-
Title XX era, CASP plans remain deficient in many respects.  As noted, CASP
planning is heavily dependent upon the decisions made in the state budgetary
process.  Similarly, where programs have been locked-in when the state agency
has reached its ceiling, the CASP becomes more of a scorecard than a plan.

   Plans, too, are commonly understood to include timetables for the
realization of specific and measurable objectives.  In most instances,
state CASP plans do not specify more than which categories of persons are
to be provided which types of services.  Most CASP plans, then, focus on
means (i.e., services to be provided) rather than ends (i.e., what results
are expected from the provision of services to specific populations).

   Finally, there is no provision for feedback of prior-period performance
or even comparison of proposed allocations with past distributions of resources.
Similarly, it is difficult for would-be participants to form an opinion on a
proposed CASP plan when the difference between what is proposed and what exists
is not made explicit.

   The CASP plan was originally envisioned as a comprehensive plan.  That is,
statute and regulations apparently conceived of the CASP plan as reflecting the
totality of a state's social services program.  However, there are several disincentives for states to present their total program in the CASP.  The primary
disincentive is the absence of a significant incentive to do so.  Since the
CASP plan is not accepted by HEW as the human services plan for other programs
(e.g., services for the aging, the mentally ill, and the developmentally
disabled, vocational rehabilitation services, and child welfare services).

2.  It is doubtful that the public participation experienced under
Title XX is representative of either consumers or the general population.

Members of the public who have participated in social services
priority-setting under Title XX have generally represented the special
interests of providers or particularly articulate population groups.

Although the increased involvement of non-SSD participants in social
services decision-making has been one of the major achievements of Title XX,
the imbalance of that activity is of concern in three important respects.
First, the means of representing the interests of presumably unrepresented
segments of the public are not articulated under Title XX. Second, the
relationship between the role of special interests and the role of the
elected representatives of a state's entire population (e.g., governors and
legislators) is not clear. Third, the lack of data on program needs and
service efficacy severely constrains the ability of state social services
administrators to bring any special expertise to bear on decisions which are
made in an increasingly politicized environment. Among the most notable out-
growths of this changed environment for social services priority-setting have
been (a) pressure to expand to the fullest extent permitted by the federal
ceiling in states that have not yet reached the ceiling; (b) expansion of
purchased services rather than those provided directly by the public social
services agency; (c) preferences for services which are tangible, visible,
and/or have organized constituencies in support of them; and (d) increased
pressure for equity in the substate allocation of Title XX funds.

3.  There remains an opportunity for state and federal leadership
to make Title XX something other than a "source of funds."

It remains to be seen whether Title XX will be permanently viewed as
just another source of federal funds or as the nation's social services
program.

In spite of the areas where implementation of Title XX may have thus far fallen short of expectations many held for the legislation, there exist several opportunities for state and federal leadership to improve social services planning:

o   Actions to improve the CASP as a vehicle for <u>meaningful planning</u>.

o   Actions to improve the CASP as a means of <u>comprehensive</u> human resources programming.

o   Actions to improve the <u>representativeness</u> of public participation.

o   Actions to improve our understanding of the <u>efficacy</u> of social services.

o   Actions to improve the <u>linkages</u> between CASP planning and state budgetary processes.

### III.  FINANCING SOCIAL SERVICES

A.  INTRODUCTION

In the five-year period from 1963 to 1967, federal expenditures for social services under Titles IV-A and VI of the Social Security Act grew gradually from $194.3 million per year to $281.6 million per year.  In 1967 a series of amendments to the Social Security Act relaxed many of the restrictions which the federal government had imposed on the states' ability to purchase services from other public and private agencies.  A number of states began to utilize the opportunities provided by the 1967 amendments to use federal social services funds to finance a series of programs whose relationship to the basic social services program may have been tenuous at best.

These purchases frequently involved "supplantation," a practice in which federal funds were used to replace state financial support of pre-existing government services or to finance new or expanded services that would otherwise have been fully state-funded.  The combined effects of supplantation and program development greatly accelerated the growth in federal social services costs.  While the growth rate in the five-year period prior to the 1967 amendments had ranged from 20 to 25 percent per year, between 1969 and 1971 federal costs increased sharply.  By 1972 the total federal expenditures for social services had reached $1.7 billion a year, a level twice as high as in the preceding year and nearly nine times higher than the costs had been only a decade earlier.

Under the legislation then in existence the federal funding authorizations for social services were open-ended.  This form of authorization obligated the federal government to reimburse the states for 75 percent of the costs of eligible services provided to eligible clients, regardless of the total amount expended. Consequently, the possibilities for continued uncontrolled growth were very real. Devising effective methods for national cost control in a program as varied and complex as the 51 social services systems in the United States was not a simple undertaking. Cost-control methods which will work in every jurisdiction and at the same time retain equity between the states are difficult to develop. Congress, in effect, avoided this dilemma by limiting federal social services expenditures to $2.5 billion per year and allocating these funds among the states on the basis of their general population. This action left to states the responsibility for either finding cost-control solutions or alternative funding sources.

At the time it was established in 1972, the $2.5 billion national ceiling may have appeared reasonable in relation to the then-current expenditure level of $1.7 billion. The impact of the ceiling on individual states, however, was uneven. Six states immediately found themselves spending in excess of their allocation (ceiling) the day it became effective, while other states were granted an opportunity for substantial program expansion.

The federal allocation method affected some states more than others for a number of reasons. The allocation formula, for example, did not consider that the concentration of low-income groups (the principal targets of Titles IV-A and VI) varied from state to state. Nor did the formula recognize the wide variation among states in pre-existing levels of real investment in social services. Furthermore, the formula did not allow for the reallocation of unspent funds from states that did not fully utilize their allocations to states that did. Consequently, those states that had already made commitments to services programs, but whose federal allocation under the ceiling was less than existing program costs, faced a dilemma.

Apparently because of the small number of states originally adversely affected by the imposition of the ceiling and the method of determining state allocations, the ceiling did not become a strong national issue until recently. A number of occurrences within the last five years have made the ceiling a more critical constraint than it was in 1972. Of these, the two major factors are inflation and the implementation of Title XX, the 1975 amendments to the Social Security Act.

1. Effects of Inflation

Inflation has accounted for an estimated 20 to 33 percent increase in the cost of state and local government services between 1972 and 1977. Because the federal ceiling has not been increased (except for the temporary authorization under P.L. 94-401) since it was imposed, the $2.5 billion authorization for social services set in 1972 authorized only the equivalent of a $1.7 billion to $2 billion program in 1977. For states that were not at ceiling in 1972, this reduction in the purchasing power of the federal allocation has only recently become a severe constraint. Until now, rising programmatic costs in these states could be covered by the unused existing resources. For the states that have been at ceiling since 1972, however, a ceiling which is unresponsive to inflation has meant a continual erosion of the purchasing power of social services dollars. In several of these jurisdictions the effects of the relative decline in the value of their federal allocation have been compounded by an absolute decline in direct federal support because of reductions in their relative proportion of the national population.

2. Effects of Title XX

The progressive tightening of social services funds has continued to occur at the same time that program expansion has been encouraged through the introduction of Title XX in 1975. Title XX was a complex compromise between the states and HEW over a wide range of cost, accountability, and control issues. Title XX was, in large measure, an outgrowth of what has been described as the "battle of the regulations." HEW's social services program regulations had continued to be restrictive even after the imposition of the ceiling in 1972. In 1973 HEW proposed a series of regulations which, if implemented, would have further constricted states' use of their federal social services allocation. The major constraints of the proposed 1973 regulations related to definitions of client eligibility and allowable services. A number of states argued that the overall effect of the proposed regulations would be to radically reduce, rather than contain, social services expenditures and at the same time to increase welfare dependency costs. The net effect of federal policy and the controversy over the proposed regulations was to hold aggregate state social services expenditures well below the level authorized in 1972.

Although service expansion was not necessarily the primary intent of Title XX when it was introduced in 1975, it is clear that a number of its provisions encourage this effect. Title XX changes program eligibility requirements to allow a state to serve persons whose incomes are as high as 115 percent of the state's median income. Title XX's "50 percent rule" also reduces the required proportion of service expenditures directed to the "categorically related" (i.e., AFDC, SSI, and Medicaid recipients) from 90 to 50 percent of federal expenditures. As a consequence, the legislation initially enabled (some would argue, encouraged) states to expand the population eligible for services. Similarly, the authorizations which allow states flexibility to determine the scope and nature of the services to be provided under the social services umbrella extend another opportunity for program expansion. Further, because it mandates an <u>open planning process</u> with increased citizen participation, Title XX provides a special opportunity for interest groups to place pressure on the states to utilize all of the federal funding available to them. Finally, rather than serving as a control on service expenditures in states below their ceiling, that ceiling has instead served as a benchmark or a desirable program level, in effect stimulating program expansion.

### 3. <u>State Utilization of Ceiling</u>

The pattern of state utilization of federal social services allotments is presented as table 14. In fiscal years 1972, 1973, and 1974 there were only minor changes in state claim patterns, after discounting aberrations associated with charges for prior periods. For purposes of this analysis a state is considered to fully utilize its federal allocation if it uses 95 percent or more of it. In each of these three years (1972 through 1974) only four to six states utilized their entire federal social services allocation. In 1975, however, nine more states reached their limit on federal financial participation. By 1976 a total of twenty states were at ceiling, and in 1977 over half of the states reached their ceilings. HEW estimates suggest that the ceiling will become a constraint for nearly all jurisdictions within the next two years. Further, because the states already at ceiling represent most of the largest states (measured by their combined proportion of the total Title XX appropriation), the effect of the ceiling on the nation's social services program is already extensive.

The actual impact of the ceiling may be even more significant than these data indicate simply because states make decisions on the basis of their perceived relationship to their ceiling. States approaching their ceiling, for example, are often unwilling to undertake new program initiatives which may not be sustainable a year or two in the future.

52

# TABLE 14

## State Percent Utilization of Federal Social Services Allocations, Fiscal Years 1972-1977

| | 1972 | 1973 [a,b] | 1974 [b] | 1975 [b] | 1976 | 1977 |
|---|---|---|---|---|---|---|
| Alabama | 28 | 40 | 48 | 58 | 71 | 84 |
| Alaska | 108 | 151 | 79 | 79 | 100 | 99 |
| Arizona | 12 | 14 | 13 | 16 | 26 | 80 |
| Arkansas | 14 | 26 | 23 | 37 | 49 | 74 |
| California | 81 | 93 | 95 | 100 | 100 | 90 |
| Colorado | 67 | 78 | 88 | 100 | 100 | 90 |
| Connecticut | 25 | 56 | 103 | 100 | 100 | 100 |
| Delaware | 184 | 97 | 72 | 86 | 94 | 89 |
| District of Columbia | 117 | 92 | 98 | 99 | 100 | 100 |
| Florida | 49 | 50 | 33 | 153 | 97 | 100 |
| Georgia | 57 | 85 | 64 | 81 | 92 | 95 |
| Hawaii | 9 | 24 | 63 | 84 | 83 | 95 |
| Idaho | 17 | 52 | 73 | 100 | 100 | 87 |
| Illinois | 140 | 91 | 64 | 60 | 70 | 68 |
| Indiana | 10 | 11 | 11 | 9 | 14 | 28 |
| Iowa | 28 | 37 | 45 | 71 | 100 | 100 |
| Kansas | 23 | 26 | 28 | 47 | 65 | 92 |
| Kentucky | 32 | 77 | 63 | 123 | 100 | 97 |
| Louisiana | 66 | 47 | 46 | 52 | 71 | 86 |
| Maine | 52 | 70 | 53 | 62 | 83 | 88 |
| Maryland | 43 | 55 | 61 | 78 | 91 | 96 |
| Massachusetts | 33 | 24 | 42 | 75 | 93 | 100 |
| Michigan | 26 | 44 | 84 | 83 | 95 | 100 |
| Minnesota | 57 | 65 | 88 | 116 | 100 | 100 |
| Mississippi | 7 | 43 | 19 | 23 | 31 | 63 |
| Missouri | 23 | 27 | 31 | 37 | 50 | 75 |
| Montana | 34 | 44 | 45 | 63 | 100 | 97 |
| Nebraska | 40 | 51 | 66 | 99 | 100 | 84 |
| Nevada | 26 | 28 | 36 | 48 | 59 | 75 |
| New Hampshire | 31 | 44 | 46 | 72 | 75 | 79 |
| New Jersey | 42 | 50 | 56 | 82 | 94 | 92 |
| New Mexico | 29 | 62 | 67 | 62 | 80 | 93 |
| New York | 267 | 91 | 105 | 101 | 100 | 98 |
| North Carolina | 31 | 39 | 33 | 48 | 66 | 89 |
| North Dakota | 44 | 52 | 44 | 54 | 74 | 96 |
| Ohio | 15 | 32 | 36 | 42 | 48 | 78 |
| Oklahoma | 45 | 78 | 55 | 66 | 84 | 100 |
| Oregon | 97 | 78 | 53 | 100 | 96 | 100 |
| Pennsylvania | 36 | 62 | 67 | 84 | 81 | 98 |
| Rhode Island | 57 | 81 | 92 | 91 | 100 | 100 |
| South Carolina | 19 | 31 | 36 | 58 | 85 | 87 |
| South Dakota | 29 | 30 | 19 | 43 | 79 | 100 |
| Tennessee | 29 | 49 | 32 | 36 | 58 | 70 |
| Texas | 38 | 68 | 56 | 101 | 100 | 99 |
| Utah | 30 | 41 | 41 | 57 | 75 | 99 |
| Vermont | 44 | 58 | 54 | 88 | 100 | 100 |
| Virginia | 28 | 38 | 40 | 52 | 67 | 83 |
| Washington | 83 | 137 | 103 | 97 | 100 | 100 |
| West Virginia | 35 | 38 | 49 | 63 | 91 | 100 |
| Wisconsin | 70 | 100 | 81 | 96 | 100 | 100 |
| Wyoming | 14 | 24 | 28 | 41 | 89 | 75 |
| No. of States at Ceiling [c] | 6 | 4 | 5 | 14 | 20 | 26 |

Sources: 1972--Staff Data and Materials on Social Services Regulations, Senate Finance Committee Hearings, 93d Congress, 1st Sess. (May 1973), pp. 19-21, 1973-1975--USDHEW, PSA Budget Office table, "Federal Social Services Funding Under Titles IVA, VI, and XX"; 1976--USDHEW Technical Notes 1, March 1977, p. 4 (Original source was SSR Budget Office actual use report); 1977--USDHEW, Administration for Public Services, Grants Management Branch.

a.  1973 includes adjustments related to the "hold harmless" provision of Section 1130 of the 1972 amendments.
b.  The 1973-5 data are not adjusted for chargebacks to prior fiscal year; therefore, utilization can exceed 100 percent.
c.  Ceiling is defined as utilization of 95 percent or more of the state authorization.

B.    COST CONTROL

Reliance on the comfortable assumption that limiting the total amount
spent under a specific title will automatically control costs may obscure
the extent of the activities states have undertaken to preserve service
levels and/or permit program expansion.   There are a number of ways for
states that have reached the ceiling to secure additional funds.   Social
services departments (SSDs) can appeal to state and local legislative
bodies for additional funding to meet current cost crises or to sustain
existing programs.   The departments can often look to private sources for
matching funds or independent support for services that cannot be supported
by public resources alone.   Many states already have examined, and more are
planning to examine, the entire range of federally assisted programs for
possible sources of funding for social services.

1.  State and Local Funds

Several of the eight states examined in The Urban Institute's study
have asked for and received supplementary state appropriations to support
Title XX programs beyond the ceiling level.   In one state, the supplementary
funding took the form of a cost-of-living adjustment plus funds to minimize
the effects of a new substate allocation formula.   In two states, supple-
ments to the Title XX budget have established funds for sharing the costs
of social services with the counties.   Yet another state has established
a fully state-funded social services program of special services for the
elderly.

In each of these instances, there has been a direct appeal to the
state legislature to maintain support for social service programs when
the federal funding limits are reached.   There are also instances where
more subtle approaches are taken.   One state legislature does not directly
allow the human resources department's expenditures to exceed federally

matchable levels. However, over the last three years (1975 to 1978) the SSD has reduced its purchases from other state agencies by about $26 million, thereby freeing up Title XX funds for other service programs. The matching funds for the new social services programs have largely come from state and local sources. Apparently, the other state departments which had been partially supported by Title XX funds make up the deficit by seeking state appropriations or supplementary local support. In either event, the net result has been an increase in total expenditures for services.

The funding ceiling can also be at least temporarily sidestepped by soliciting supplementary county funds. For counties without sufficient local monies to match available federal funds, a new option has been created which permits the use of General Revenue Sharing funds as the match for other federal funds. Few jurisdictions were observed to be taking advantage of this option, however.

## 2. Intertitle Transfers

Although state and local governments have been sources of additional funds, the evidence suggests that the largest actual and potential sources for additional funds have been other major national social welfare appropriations.

There are distinct financial incentives for states to consider transferring the funding sources of social services once program costs have reached or exceeded the federal funding limit under Title XX. The direction of the transfer process which characterized the period prior to 1972 has been reversed. At that time, states transferred social programs into Title IV-A and VI (Title XX's predecessors) to obtain the 75 percent match. Now, in states at ceiling, there appears to be an increasing shift of programs out of Title XX. The net effect of either of these flows is

the same:  increased federal costs.  Family planning, for example, eligible
for a 90 percent reimbursement under Title XX, is almost invariably being
moved to Title XIX in order to free Title XX to support programs for which
there would otherwise be no federal match or to absorb the growing costs of
other programs in the Title XX package.

There can be a significant advantage in accepting the lower reimbursement rates under other federal titles which may have less severe limits on
reimbursement than Title XX, rather than taking the 75 percent reimbursement
under Title XX, which has a finite allocation.  In short, 50 percent federal
funding is, understandably, preferred to none.

The key incentive for intertitle transfers is the availability of federal
funds, frequently without limits, in a number of programs which allow for
payments for services which could conceivably be funded under either title.
Given the choice, a state at ceiling would probably make a net gain by
transferring from Title XX all service programs that could be funded under
other titles to those titles and using Title XX funds for programs for which
no other federal support is available.  The major constraint on such transfers
is the difficulty of controlling costs when funds are shifted from Title XX
to an entitlement program.

Fund transfers are difficult to track even when a state explicitly
identifies them, and no systematic analysis of intertitle transfers has yet
been undertaken.  The data from the eight-state in-depth study and the survey
of senior state administrators, however, indicate that at least some inter-
title transfers are occurring in each state.

Maximization of federal funding and avoidance of social service program
cutbacks are the two major reasons given for transferring programs between
federal funding sources.  These two concerns are cited as the reasons for

over half of the current and anticipated transfers in both the ceiling and non-ceiling states (see table 15).

The respondents to the survey of senior state administrators also reported that a very wide range of federal titles other than Title XX were being used to support social services programs (see table 16). According to the survey, Titles IV-A (AFDC), IV-B (Child Welfare), IV-C (WIN), XIX (Medicaid), and IV-A and XX (Training) of the Social Security Act appear to be the major federal alternative funding sources for social services.

Title IV-A is normally considered to be an income transfer program, but because the legislation makes allowances for a number of disregards

TABLE 15

Distribution of Reasons for Current
Transfers Between Fund Sources

| Reason | Ceiling States | Non-Ceiling States | Total States |
|---|---|---|---|
| Maximize Federal Funding | 23.5 | 34.3 | 29.7 |
| Avoid Social Service Cutbacks | 22.9 | 19.2 | 20.7 |
| Promote Administrative Flexibility | 15.1 | 22.9 | 19.6 |
| Comply with Federal Requirements | 16.7 | 9.0 | 12.2 |
| Reorder Service Priorities | 11.7 | 8.6 | 9.9 |
| Minimize Audit Exceptions | 7.3 | 4.5 | 5.7 |
| Avoid Federal Requirements | 2.8 | 1.6 | 2.1 |
| Total | 100.0% | 100.0% | 100.0% |

Source:  The Urban Institute Title XX Study: Senior Social Services Administrator Survey.

Totals may not always add to 100 percent because of rounding.

## TABLE 16

## Fund Source Transfers

| | Percent of Responses Indicating Programs Are Being Transferred from the Fund Source | | | | Percent of Responses Indicating Programs Are Being Transferred to the Fund Source | | | |
| | Ceiling States | | Non-Ceiling States | | Ceiling States | | Non-Ceiling States | |
| | Sen. Adm. Survey | 8 State In-Depth St. | Sen. Adm. Survey | 8 State In-Depth St. | Sen. Adm. Survey | 8 State In-Depth St. | Sen. Adm. Survey | 8 State In-Depth St. |
|---|---|---|---|---|---|---|---|---|
| **Federal Fund Sources** | | | | | | | | |
| Title XX | 44.8 | 78.6 | 23.6 | 7.1 | 55.2 | 21.8 | 76.4 | 84.2 |
| Title XIX | 2.1 | 1.2 | 2.3 | - | 6.7 | 39.2 | 3.8 | 5.3 |
| Title IV-A | 6.7 | 2.4 | 5.3 | - | 7.2 | 12.6 | 1.8 | - |
| Title IV-B | 4.6 | - | 8.6 | - | 7.2 | 2.3 | 2.3 | - |
| Title IV-C | 0.5 | - | 5.1 | - | 6.7 | 1.1 | 4.1 | - |
| Title III & VII | 3.6 | 1.2 | 5.1 | 42.9 | 5.1 | 2.3 | 1.5 | - |
| Trng. (IV-A & XX) | 9.8 | - | 6.9 | - | 4.6 | 2.3 | 4.8 | - |
| Subtotal Federal | 72.1 | 83.4 | 56.9 | 50.0 | 92.7 | 81.5 | 94.7 | 89.5 |
| **Other Fund Sources** | | | | | | | | |
| State | 13.9 | 7.1 | 13.5 | 35.7 | 3.1 | 10.3 | 2.3 | -- |
| Local | 6.2 | n.c. | 14.5 | - | 1.5 | n.c. | 1.0 | -- |
| Donated | 7.7 | n.c. | 13.2 | - | 2.6 | n.c. | 1.5 | -- |
| Other | - | 9.5 | 2.0 | 14.3 | - | 8.0 | 0.5 | 10.5 |
| Subtotal Other | 27.8 | 16.6 | 43.2 | 50.0 | 7.2 | 18.3 | 5.3 | 10.5 |
| Total | 100.0 | 100.0 | 100.0 | 100.0 | 100.0 | 100.0 | 100.0 | 100.0 |

Note: Totals do not always add up to 100% because of rounding.

or special needs, some states have found it advantageous to transfer day care services for AFDC recipients from Title XX to IV-A. Title IV-B is a separate section of the Social Security Act which specifically provides funds for child welfare services. Even though IV-B is a small, closed-ended appropriation, the fact that there are only minimal restrictions on its use allows states to transfer services ineligible for Title XX funds into IV-B and to transfer services eligible for Title XX funds from IV-B to Title XX. Title IV-C is more commonly known as the WIN (Work Incentive) program. WIN has an closed-ended fund authorization, and provides 90 percent reimbursement for services that enable AFDC clients to participate in employment and training programs. Through judicious use of Titles IV-B and IV-C, a state can better comply with the 50 percent rule.

Title XIX is an open-ended medical assistance program, but its provisions for supportive services have enabled a number of states to charge the social services provided to clients who are eligible for Medicaid benefits to that program, rather than to Title XX. Family planning and homemaker/chore services are the most commonly mentioned social services whose costs have been moved from Title XX to Title XIX. The range of optional funding sources within HEW is suggested in table 17.

The possible sources of funds a state can consider when contemplating program transfers which have been mentioned so far are all under the control of HEW. But the states are not arbitrarily limited to HEW programs. As the Child Welfare League of America/Hecht Institute points out, there are over 60 programs for children's services alone, scattered among various HEW offices and other federal government departments. Community Development Block Grants (administered by the Department of Housing and Urban Development), school lunch programs (administered by the Department of Agriculture), and the

TABLE 17

Scope of Major National Social Service Programs, FY 1977

| Program | Major Eligible Services | Basic Federal Share | Type of Appropriation | Estimated Expenditures (in Millions) | | | Est. No. of Persons Served |
|---|---|---|---|---|---|---|---|
| | | | | Federal | Non-Federal | Total | |
| **General Social Services:** | | | | | | | |
| Title XX, Social Security Act | General Services | 75 | Closed | $2,400 | $750 | $3,150 | 5,900,000/yr. |
| | Training & Retraining | 75 | Open | | | | |
| | Family Planning | 90 | Closed | | | | |
| Title XX, Social Security Act | Family Planning | 50 | Open | n.a. | n.a. | n.a. | n.a. |
| | Homemaker/Home Health | | | | | | |
| **Services to Children, Youth & Families** | | | | | | | |
| Title IV-A, Social Security Act | Foster Care, Day Care | 50 | Open | 271 | 155 | 426 | 104,000/mo. |
| Title IV-B, Social Security Act | Child Welfare | 100 | Closed | 57 | 696 | 735 | 200,000 |
| Title IV-C, Social Security Act | Employment Related | 90 | Closed | 370 | 370 | 740 | 1,000,000 |
| Title I, P.L. 93-644: Head Start | Developmental Services | 80 | Closed | 475 | 90 | 565 | 349,000 |
| Title III, Juvenile Justice Act | Runaway Youth Houses | 90 | Closed | 8 | 1 | 9 | 60,000 |
| Child Abuse Prevention/Treatment | Child Welfare | 100 | Closed | 19 | – | 19 | n.a. |
| **Services to the Aging** | | | | | | | |
| Title II, Older Americans | State & Community Services | 75 | Closed | 187 | 63 | 250 | 1,300,000 |
| Title V, Older Americans Act | Senior Citizens Center | 75 | Closed | 20 | 6 | 26 | n.a. |
| Title VII, Older Americans Act | Nutrition | 90 | Closed | 204 | 20 | 224 | 530,000/day |
| **Services to the Disabled** | | | | | | | |
| Rehabilitation Act of 1973 | Gen. Rehabilitation Services | 80 | Closed | 881 | 189 | 1,070 | 1,800,000/yr. |
| | Social Security Beneficiaries | 100 | | | | | |
| Dev. Disab. & Bill of Rts. Act | Coord. Services to Dev. Disabled | 75 | Closed | 58 | 19 | 77 | 69,000/yr. |
| Comm. Mental Health (P.L. 94-63) | State/Community Mental Health | 30-75[a] | Closed | 80 | n.a. | 80 | 530,000/day |
| **Services to Native Americans** | | | | | | | |
| Title VIII of P.L. 93-644 | Services to Indians | 80[b] | Closed | 33 | 6 | 39 | n.a. |
| | | | | $5,063 | $2,365 | $7,428 | |

Note: "n.a." indicates that data were not available

a. Non-federal share may be lower in poverty areas.

b. Non-federal share may be waived.

Comprehensive Employment and Training Act (administered by the Department of Labor), are some of the more obvious sources of funds outside HEW. Federal social services programs, both within and outside HEW, have different national goals, various methods of operation, and separate policy guidelines and regulations. Under these circumstances, the potential for weakened federal control and perversion of federal policy intent is obvious, should the states-- as they appear to be doing--consider avoidance of federal oversight a major factor in program transfer decisions.

C.   LESSONS FROM P.L. 94-401

One aspect of the Title XX experience may be particularly instructive to those who would modify national policy governing the ceiling on federal social services expenditures. On September 7, 1976, President Ford signed into law P.L. 94-401, an amendment to Title XX, granting to states an additional $240 million for child care programs from that time to October 1, 1977. The stated purposes of the additional funding were to assist states in the effort to upgrade child care standards, to comply with the Federal Inter-agency Day Care Requirements (FIDCR), and to provide full federal funding for the cost of employing welfare recipients in child care jobs (up to $5,000 per employee). Although the actual use of these funds has not been determined, preliminary data indicate that 20 states, representing nearly three-fifths of the nation's social services program, may not have used the majority of those funds in ways apparently intended by the legislation. In these states, P.L. 94-401 funds were substituted for funds previously allocated for child care. This supplantation freed funds for use in other program areas, often resulting in little or no actual expansion of day care services.

1.  Factors Favoring Supplantation

Certain factors can be identified which may have influenced state

decisions on the use of P.L. 94-401 funds. In retrospect, at least, it

appears that the majority of these factors support state use of the funds

for purposes other than those apparently intended by Congress. Such factors

include:

o Absence of maintenance of effort. The most significant aspect

of 94-401 was the absence of a "maintenance of effort" provision (i.e., a

stipulation that states could not concurrently reduce their existing programs

and substitute in their place newly appropriated funds). Maintenance of

state effort in social services progams had been an area of contention in

federal-state relations from 1970 to 1975. Although it was recognized that

drafting maintenance of effort provisions which states (were they so inclined)

could not maneuver around would have been difficult if not impossible, the

absence of any stipulation apparently signalled to many state officials that

they could choose where to apply the additional funds authorized by P.L. 94-401.

o Late issuance of regulations. Many state officials are reluctant

to implement legislation before agency regulations are issued. By the time HEW

issued the regulations in their "interim final" form, six months of the period

for which funding had been authorized had lapsed.

o Inadequate lead time. Whether or not state officials waited for

firm regulations, they generally needed time to decide how to use 94-401 funds.

And, where proposed state use of those funds involved contracting, personnel

procedures, or liaison with locally administered or privately provided services,

these actions had to be set in motion.

o Legislative and executive involvement. In a few instances it

was reported that the legislature or chief executive of the state overruled

a social service agency's decision to use the P.L. 94-401 funds for day care.

o   <u>Reluctance to engage in one-time-only programs</u>.   Since 94-401
was a temporary authorization, several state agencies and private providers
were reluctant to hire clients and make commitments to expand programs which
might not be sustainable as a result of the $2.5 billion ceiling on annual
Title XX appropriations.

o   <u>Constraints on staffing and expenditures</u>.   A few state
agencies are effectively precluded from hiring additional staff or undertaking significantly expanded expenditures without prior legislative
and/or executive approval.   Some state budgetary processes do not permit
states to accept federal funds without undergoing a time-consuming review
process.

o   <u>Fiscal constraints</u>.   One major influence on state's use of
P.L. 94-401 funds is the "fiscal crunch" they are experiencing.   Virtually
all of the large urbanized states at their ceiling are believed to have
utilized most of their P.L. 94-401 funds for purposes other than day care.

o   <u>Disproportionate funding</u>.   The portion of the basic Title XX
allocation already devoted to day care may be another factor influencing
state decisions on the use of P.L. 94-401 funds.   Where it is believed that
social services funds have traditionally been disproportionately devoted to
child care, state officials may be reluctant to allocate additional funds to
this program.

o   <u>Title XX as a source of funds</u>.   A recurring theme of this paper
is that many states view Title XX as a source of funds rather than a program
to attain specific objectives.   States that view Title XX primarily as a funding source tend to design their social services programs to meet their own
needs, rather than to conform with federal legislative intent.   As federal funds
become available (as they did with 94-401) during a program period, they are
merely absorbed or treated as an accounting, rather than a policy, issue.

o     Perceived flexibility.  State and regional offices' perspectives on the appropriate or permitted use of 94-401 funds vary widely.
To the extent that a state perceives an option, it may be more likely to
exercise one.

2.  Factors favoring the use of funds for day care

Although this discussion has centered on the "diversion" of P.L. 94-401
funds, the majority of states apparently used those funds for child care.
Some of the factors which may have influenced a state to utilize the 94-401
funds for day care include:

o     "Foot in the Door."  To some state officials, the availability of one-time-only funding presented an opportunity rather than a
limitation.  In these instances, state officials may essentially gamble
that either additional follow-on 94-401 or equivalent funds will be
available or that their state legislatures will be reluctant to cut back
on an existing program.

o     Active and articulate interests.  The passage of P.L. 94-401
was accomplished at least in part as a result of a national network of
active and articulate interests.  In many instances, local counterpart
agencies were alerted and were active early on in monitoring state use of
the 94-401 funds.

o     Congressional intent.  In some states, officials perceived that
their only option was to utilize the funds in the manner intended by Congress.
In these states, 94-401 funds were likely to be spent on child care.

o     Inadequate funding.  States that considered the funding of
their child care programs to be inadequate prior to 94-401 were more likely
to spend the additional funds for child care programs, even if they were aware
of other options open to them.

D.    <u>CONCLUSION</u>

1. <u>The ceiling on Federal Title XX expenditures may not have halted</u>
<u>the growth of program costs borne by either federal or non-federal sources</u>.

It is difficult to assess the relative importance--in terms of cost
value--of the major national programs other than Title XX which can be
used to finance social services.  However, some of the background data
collected in the eight-state in-depth study suggest that the magnitude
of these transfers can be substantial.  The estimated cost to the federal
government of just the transfers contemplated in the eight study states
is $303.7 million--$151.4 million to Title IV-A and $152.3 million to
Title XIX.  Moreover, it is not anticipated that transfers would result
in a savings to the Title XX program.  It is expected that states that
have exceeded their ceiling will use the funds made available by the
transfers to support services for which they currently bear full funding
responsibility and that other states will use the funds to expand other
Title XX services.

In cases where other federal programs can be used as funding sources,
the Title XX expenditure ceiling has not capped Federal social services
expenditures.  It would appear, too, that transfer process can result in
a substantial demand for additional state or other non-federal funds to
finance the matching portions of the expanded service program.

2. <u>The ceiling on social services expenditures may have reduced federal</u>
<u>influence over social services programming</u>.

Since the passage of the Social Security Act, federal influence over state
social services programs has largely been predicated upon the financial incentives
provided by the national grant programs.

Under Title XX, financial incentives lose much of their strength when
a state reaches its ceiling on federal social services funding.  Not only is

there little inducement to undertake new or expanded programs, but federal financial participation in existing service programs is also reduced. Further, as more and more states are able to shift programs into and out of Title XX at will, the impact of federal requirements (e.g., FIDCR and the 50 percent rule) and audit exceptions within Title XX is diminished.

The overwhelming majority of state respondents (83.3 percent) conclude that a loss in federal leverage over state social services programs has already occurred as a direct consequence of the ceiling. It is interesting that few (26.7 percent) of the regional office respondents have perceived any current reduction in federal leverage as a consequence of the ceiling (see table 18).

3. State and/or local control over social services programming appears to have been enhanced by Title XX.

The federal expenditures ceiling imposed under Title XX seems to have concurrently increased state social services departments' control over social services programs in some respects and decreased it in others. Increased state control seems to be a product of the opportunities offered by inter-title transfers and by the imposition of service mandates and program guidelines on substate jurisdictions because of fiscal pressures. Some decline in state SSD autonomy appears to be the result of the larger roles being played by state legislatures and budget bureaus when critical decisions concerning funding allocations are made.

In every state examined, program levels varied substantially from county to county, often because of differences among the counties in their ability to provide matching funds. As program costs have increased because of the combined effects of inflation and real growth, counties that formerly used relatively small proportions of the available funds are now demanding their "fair share" of the total limited resources under Title XX. As a result, a

TABLE 18

Impact of Ceiling on Federal Program Control

### Impact of Ceiling--Loss of Federal Leverage?

|  | % Yes | % No |
|---|---|---|
| Impact to Date: | | |
| 8-State Responses | 83.3 | 16.7 |
| Regional Office Responses | 26.7 | 73.3 |
| Anticipated Impact: | | |
| 8-State Responses | 100.0 | 0 |
| Regional Office Responses | 34.4 | 65.7 |

Note:  Totals may not always add to 100 percent because of rounding.

growing number of states have established allocation formulae based on such factors as general population, low-income population, categorical population, and past expenditure history.  Where these formulae are enduring and cover most of the services program, local authority over social services programming may be enhanced at the expense of the state.

4.  Any increments to the Title XX ceiling should be made in light of experience with P.L. 94-401

Several alternative proposals to raise the Title XX ceiling have been advanced.  Some would target funds within the Title XX pool to particular populations or programs (e.g., Native Americans, residents of urban areas, or child welfare programs).  Others would increase the overall $2.5 billion authorization to offset, at least partially, the effects of inflation. Although clear statements of federal intent may be helpful in promoting

the consistent use of increments to the ceiling, it is doubted that any
meaningful maintenance of effort provision would be effective in an area
as nebulously defined as social services.

State experiences with P.L. 94-401 funds argue that any increments to
the Title XX ceiling should:

o   Provide adequate lead time for the desired policy and pro-
    grammatic changes to be planned and implemented.

o   Be timed to allow incorporation of the change into the
    planning and participative elements of each state's CASP
    planning cycle.

o   Be authorized on a permanent (rather than a one-time-only)
    basis if a continuing expansion in state service programs is
    contemplated.

## IV. ALLOCATING SOCIAL SERVICES RESOURCES

### A. INTRODUCTION

In addition to describing the process shifts effected by Title XX, this paper attempts to describe the extent to which those shifts have changed the allocation of social services resources. Inevitably, this analysis is limited in two major respects. First, a number of factors other than Title XX's implementation affect social services priority-setting. Second, the data available are, in almost every instance, fragmentary. Nevertheless, they do suggest some of the major shifts in the allocation of resources which may have stemmed from the Title XX experience. Before focusing on these changes, however, some discussion of the factors inhibiting change is appropriate.

#### 1. Ceiling

The most significant federal limitation placed on resource allocation under Title XX is the retention of the $2.5 billion ceiling imposed in 1972. The states which had reached their ceiling prior to the introduction of Title XX found that their flexibility under Title XX was limited by the political and practical difficulty in reallocating funds which had already been committed to other services. As more states reach their ceiling, this legislative limitation is expected increasingly to constrain the resource allocation process.

#### 2. Matching Funds

The federal legislation also retained the requirement that states provide the 25 percent matching funds in order to obtain reimbursement for basic Title XX service expenditures. Obtaining matching funds continues to be a problem in a number of states, particularly where the SSD is dependent on local government contributions or donated funds. In states that depend on non-state sources to generate matching funds, service allocation patterns are often affected by the preferences of those other parties in the use of Title XX funds. This dependency on non-state non/federal funds tends to inhibit the ability of state agencies to reorder service priorities.

3. Nature of Federal Mandates

Although the Title XX legislation implicitly assumes that the distribution of services will be affected by encouraging public input into the planning process and requiring service needs assessment, this assumption remains untested. Title XX does not mandate a form of public participation guaranteed to produce change, and it does not impose any penalty on states that do not change their plans based on the input they receive. Furthermore, the legislation sets no standards pertaining to the quality or comprehensiveness of the needs assessment process, nor does it require that the findings be used in setting service or target population priorities.

4. CASP/Budget Linkages

State and local budgets for social services have also placed limitations on the pattern of service expenditures. The divergence between CASP planning cycles and state and local budget schedules initially prevented major reallocations under Title XX. Most states continue to have this problem. The levels at which the budgets are set may be an even greater constraint on resource allocation than the CASP planning process.

5. Lack of Objective Data

In order to "rationally" effect changes in service patterns, it may be necessary (but not always sufficient) to have objective data which can be used to justify the changes being proposed. One of the major impediments to change that states face is the unavailability of such data and the low level of analysis undertaken in examining them.

### 6.  Limited Use of Needs Assessments

While the majority of states have undertaken some form of statewide needs assessments, there are various definitions of needs assessments, ranging from informal polls of SSD management to surveys measuring demand for particular services.  On the whole, the assessments have suffered from the unreliability of the data, the difficulty of measuring demand but not supply, and the inability to compare demand and supply.  Additionally, it may be argued that what has, in the past, passed for needs assessment may not, in fact, be a sound basis for policy-making.

### 7.  Divergence Between Planned and Actual Performance

The assumption that planning for changes in services would necessarily result in real change has also proven to have limited validity under Title XX.  While the HEW regional offices believed that actual performance in two-thirds of the states would not deviate from planned service levels, the experience of the majority of the eight states examined closely by The Urban Institute clearly indicates that the plan does not govern the pattern of actual services provided.  In addition, few states have the means to monitor the implementation of their plans to determine whether or not actual service patterns are consistent with the plans.

### 8.  Limitations Imposed by Politics and Public Participation

The expectation that significant resource allocation changes will occur as a result of the Title XX public planning process is based on the assumption that public input is, to a large degree, political and that it results in change.  Expectations of change, too, stem from the belief that the nature of public participation under Title XX would differ from that which had previously existed (i.e., would not support the status quo).

It should be noted that the true pattern of social services resource allocation under Title XX is obscured by changes in both federal and state program fund sources. A more detailed explanation of the effects of these funding changes is presented in chapter III. The subject is mentioned here because of the need to emphasize that the resource allocation patterns reviewed in this chapter may reflect both real changes in service distribution resulting from Title XX and spurious changes resulting from transfers of social services out of Title XX.

B.    CHANGES IN THE ALLOCATION OF RESOURCES AMONG SERVICES

In both the eight-state interviews and the 51-jurisdiction survey of HEW regional offices, respondents' perceptions of the changes in services which had occurred under Title XX were obtained (see table 19). While the majority of respondents indicated that there was no overall change in the pattern of services, there were some interesting variations in the responses.

The regional office respondents, based on their review of the services provided in the 51 states, indicated a greater positive change for education and training, transportation, and home management services than was observed by the respondents in the eight-state study. The eight-state respondents, in contrast, perceived a greater positive impact for health-related services under Title XX than the regional office respondents indicated. The majority of both groups, however, agreed that Title XX had had the greatest positive impact in the children's protective service category.

Title XX was perceived to have had the greatest negative impact on counseling services, although this perception was held only by the eight-state respondents. The varying degree to which the change in counseling services may be related to the presumed increases in caseworkers' administrative duties under Title XX, the increase in purchased services (counseling is not generally purchased), or an actual reorientation of caseworker service functions would be an interesting question to examine further.

TABLE 19

Respondents' Perceptions of Services
Affected by Title XX Implementation

| Service | 8-State Responses[a] | | | 51-Jurisdiction Responses[b] | | |
|---|---|---|---|---|---|---|
| | % Negative | % No Change | % Positive | % Negative | % No Change | % Positive |
| Protective Services (Child) | 6.4 | 34.0 | 59.6 | -0- | 51.0 | 49.0 |
| Day Care (Child) | 18.0 | 31.1 | 50.8 | 10.0 | 42.0 | 48.0 |
| Counseling | 22.6 | 58.1 | 19.3 | 3.9 | 76.5 | 19.6 |
| Foster Care (Child) | 9.4 | 53.1 | 37.5 | 2.0 | 62.7 | 35.3 |
| Homemaker | 11.1 | 42.2 | 46.7 | 2.0 | 51.0 | 47.1 |
| Health-Related | 13.8 | 48.3 | 37.9 | 3.9 | 68.6 | 27.5 |
| Education Training | 14.3 | 76.2 | 9.5 | 5.9 | 72.5 | 21.6 |
| Family Planning | 6.1 | 51.5 | 42.4 | 2.0 | 56.9 | 41.2 |
| Transportation | 13.9 | 62.1 | 24.1 | 2.0 | 58.8 | 37.3 |
| Home Management | 16.7 | 66.7 | 16.7 | 5.9 | 62.7 | 27.4 |

Note: Percentages may not always add up to 100 because of rounding.

a. The Urban Institute Title XX Study: 8 State In-Depth Study
b. The Urban Institute Title XX Study: HEW Regional Office Survey

According to the survey of regional offices, Title XX's most negative impact was on day care services, although only 10 percent of the 51 jurisdictions held this belief. Almost half of the jurisdictions indicated that Title XX has had a positive impact on day care services. The eight-state respondents exhibited a similar mix of opinion regarding Title XX's effect on day care. Almost twice as many (18 percent) of the state respondents believed that its impact has been negative, although the majority believed its impact has been generally positive. It would be interesting to determine the reasons for this variation in opinion and their relative importance. Several possible explanations follow.

o The FIDCR requirements could be construed as a constraint on day care expansion.

o In a number of states, day care programs rely heavily on local and donated support for matching funds. Although Title XX has expanded the opportunities for using these funds, it has not reduced the matching level required.

o Day care programs were singled out by Congress to receive financial support above the Title XX ceiling.

o Day care is one of the major services which have undergone fund source transfers, and these transfers could be obscuring the real impact of Title XX in this area.

In some ways, it is not surprising that the overall impression of the respondents was that Title XX has not affected services in an overwhelmingly and consistently positive way. One quarter of all the concerns expressed by the eight study states about the negative elements of Title XX pertained to the lack of change in services patterns. However, this lack of change is not expected to persist. Most of the eight-state responses (75.6 percent) and the regional office observations in all 51 jurisdictions (92.6 percent) indicated that in the future a reordering of service priorities will occur as the financial constraints of the ceiling increase.

The most interesting questions are how the redistribution of services will be achieved and what the pattern of Title XX services will look like. States at ceiling did not tend to utilize their needs assessment data for Title XX planning to any greater extent than the non-ceiling states. Overall, the major factors affecting resource decision-making were past experience, mandated services, need and available match (see table 20).

Matching funds and need were not significant factors in the service allocation process in the ceiling states. Experience and state legislative mandates operating within the constraints of the ceiling have had major effects on their service patterns.

Service priorities were also being imposed by linking service provision to the level of available funds. One cost-control method used is to restrict all but two services to levels which can be funded by the available federal and state match. Only information and referral and protective services for children must be provided regardless of financial constraints. Another means of controlling costs is to establish priorities for certain client groups within the service categories. Lower-priority groups cannot be served if the higher-ranking groups utilize the fund allocation for that service.

## C.  CHANGES IN ALLOCATION OF RESOURCES AMONG CLIENT GROUPS

The inclusion of the "income eligible" population, the "50 percent rule," and the expansion of purchased services under Title XX create a potential for changing the composition of the client population. References in predecessor legislation to "former" and "potential" recipients of federal categorical programs have been deleted and replaced with references to:

> o  "Categorically-related" recipients--recipients of AFDC, SSI, and Medical Assistance.

> o  "Income eligible" recipients--persons not categorically related but whose incomes are below maximum levels set by the state up to a maximum of 115 percent of the state's median income

TABLE 20

Services Allocation Criteria

| Criteria | Ceiling State Responses | | Non-Ceiling State Responses | |
|---|---|---|---|---|
| | Number/Percent | | Number/Percent | |
| Past Experience | 16 | 17.8 | 2 | 7.7 |
| Mandated Services | 15 | 16.7 | 2 | 7.7 |
| No Specific Criteria | 14 | 15.6 | 2 | 7.7 |
| Need | 8 | 8.9 | 5 | 19.2 |
| Negotiations Within SSD | 7 | 7.8 | 2 | 7.7 |
| Available Match | 2 | 2.2 | 5 | 19.2 |
| Negotiations Outside SSD | 3 | 3.3 | 2 | 7.7 |
| Availability of Services | 2 | 2.2 | 1 | 3.8 |
| Population Demographics | 2 | 2.2 | 1 | 3.8 |
| Line Items in Budget | 2 | 2.2 | 0 | - |
| Other | 19 | 21.1 | 4 | 15.3 |
| | 90 | 100.0% | 26 | 100.0% |

Source:  Eight State In-Depth Study

o  <u>"Without regard to income" recipients</u>--recipients of information
   and referral services and protective services.

Actual changes in the service population since Title XX are difficult

to measure because of a variety of methodological problems including limita-

tions in state reporting systems, problems in redetermination of eligibility,

and inability to identify the characteristics of the clients served as

"former" and "potential" recipients.

The March 1977 edition of HEW's <u>Technical Notes</u> reported that the trend

among states was to reduce eligiblity levels from the prior Title XX planning

period.  A review of the changes in eligibility standards which have been made

since the first Title XX planning period indicated that only seven states

significantly expanded eligibility.  Each of these states was substantially

below its federal ceiling at the time Title XX was implemented.  Sixteen states

have made mixed adjustments to their eligibility standards, tightening some and

relaxing others.  Twenty-one states have clearly restricted the service popula-

tion by reducing income eligibility levels, by adding categorical requirements,

or varying eligibility by some combination of service, client, and geographic

factors.  Of the 21 states which have reduced eligibility in these ways, 2 were

already at ceiling when Title XX was implemented, and 12 have reached their

ceiling since then.  All of the other states which have begun to reduce eligi-

bility levels have greatly increased in their utilization of federal allocations

since the implementation of Title XX.

Approximately three-fourths of the respondents in ceiling and non-ceiling

states agree that a major criterion used to determine eligibility levels is

whether those levels restrict costs to available resources (see Table 21).  The

ceiling states, in particular, are trying to maintain the scope of the old

program (by insuring that those clients are served) while responding to one of

TABLE 21

## Criteria for Setting Title XX Income Eligibility Levels

| Criteria | Percent "Yes" Response — Ceiling States | Percent "Yes" Response — Non-ceiling States | Percent Distribution of Criteria — Ceiling States | Percent Distribution of Criteria — Non-ceiling States |
|---|---|---|---|---|
| **Program Maintenance Reasons** | | | | |
| To ensure service to clients served under Titles IV-A and VI | 100.0 | 95.6 | 20.7 | 19.8 |
| **Cost Containment Reasons** | | | | |
| To restrict costs to available resources | 70.9 | 75.9 | 14.2 | 15.4 |
| To restrict eligibility to smallest number of persons | 12.1 | 5.4 | 2.5 | 1.1 |
| | | | Subtotal: 16.7 | 16.5 |
| **Restrictive Policy Reasons** | | | | |
| To restrict eligibility to the categorically related groups | 9.6 | 17.4 | 1.8 | 3.4 |
| To restrict eligibility to the lowest income groups | 32.7 | 47.7 | 6.9 | 9.6 |
| To discourage use of particular services | 13.5 | 6.4 | 1.1 | 1.3 |
| To discourage use by particular client groups | 5.8 | 2.8 | 2.5 | 0.5 |
| | | | Subtotal: 12.3 | 14.8 |
| **Expansion Policy Reasons** | | | | |
| To maximize the number of income eligibles | 70.1 | 62.9 | 14.9 | 13.2 |
| To encourage use of particular services | 59.3 | 55.8 | 11.6 | 11.4 |
| To encourage use by particular client groups | 49.1 | 44.0 | 9.5 | 8.7 |
| | | | Subtotal: 36.0 | 33.3 |
| To avoid imposing fees | 43.6 | 49.5 | 8.7 | 10.0 |
| Other | 42.9 | 40.5 | 5.5 | 5.4 |
| | | | Subtotal: 14.2 | 15.4 |
| | | | TOTAL: 100.0% | 100.0% |

Source: The Urban Institute Title XX Study: Senior Social Services Administrator Survey

Note: Totals may not always add up to 100 because of rounding.

the major objectives of Title XX (extending services to the non-categorical low-income population). They are less inclined than the non-ceiling states to restrict eligibility to the lowest-income and categorical groups, as measured by the relative difference in the percentage of respondents identifying those criteria as major factors in determining eligibility levels. The general conclusion which can be made from the data on eligibility criteria is that the states are not willing to totally sacrifice their service policies to the pressures of financial constraints. Instead, they are trying, not always successfully, to strike a balance between fiscal concerns and positive program objectives.

Caseworkers in 19 states were asked how the transition from income eligibility levels under Titles IV-A and VI to those currently in force had affected their caseloads. Their responses appear in table 22. The majority of caseworkers who expressed an opinion generally reached the following conclusions:

o There has been a continuation of service to persons who received services under Titles VI-A and VI.

o There has not been a reduction in the total number of persons receiving social services.

o There has not been a restriction in the provision of social services to persons with the lowest incomes.

o There has been an increase in the number of income eligibles receiving social services.

The passage of P.L. 93-647, Title XX of the Social Security Act, symbolized the coalescence of many divergent interests. As is often the case with major legislation, conflicting interpretations and expectations with regard to Title XX were often glossed over or left to be resolved during the law's implementation by state and local governments. One area of conflict involved Title XX's effect on the allocation of publicly

TABLE 22

Effect of Current Title XX Income Eligibility
Levels on Service Worker Caseloads

|  | Frequency | | | Percent | | |
|---|---|---|---|---|---|---|
|  | Yes | No | Don't Know | Yes | No | Don't Know |
| Continuation of services to persons who received services under Titles IV-A and VI | 102 | 21 | 98 | 46 | 10 | 44 |
| Increase in the number of income eligibles receiving social services | 95 | 49 | 79 | 43 | 22 | 35 |
| Reduction in the total number of persons receiving social services | 34 | 110 | 78 | 15 | 50 | 35 |
| Restriction in the provision of social services to the categorically related | 48 | 74 | 96 | 22 | 34 | 44 |
| Restriction in the provision of social services to persons with the lowest incomes | 35 | 108 | 77 | 16 | 49 | 35 |
| Limitation of eligibility to persons with incomes below 80% of the state's median income | 27 | 63 | 130 | 12 | 29 | 59 |
| Expanded use of particular social services (e.g., day care) | 88 | 47 | 85 | 40 | 21 | 39 |
| Reduced use of particular social services | 50 | 80 | 90 | 23 | 36 | 41 |
| Expanded use of social services by particular client populations (e.g., aging) | 75 | 44 | 102 | 34 | 20 | 46 |
| Reduced use of social services by particular client populations (e.g., aging) | 22 | 89 | 107 | 10 | 41 | 49 |
| Other | 8 | 13 | 62 | 10 | 16 | 75 |

Source:   The Urban Institute Title XX Study:  Social Service Workers Survey.

funded social services to particular sub-groups of the population such as women, minorities, and the aged.

### 1. Effects on Women and Minorities

Two questions will be examined in an attempt to assess the impact of Title XX on women and minorities:

o   Which elements of Title XX policy favor or limit the provision of social services to or by minorities and women?

o   What effects, if any, has state implementation of Title XX had on the allocation of social services to women and minorities?

As has been mentioned previously, because of Title XX's newness, hard data about its implementation were in many instances not available. Even if these data had been available, extrapolation of state-specific observations to the national experience may not have been appropriate. What was available was qualitative data in the form of interviews representing a wide variety of perspectives (e.g., intergovernmental, private, public, consumer, and provider) and quantitative data in a few states. It is hoped that the qualitative and quantitative data gathered, in spite of their limitations, will contribute to a more informed discussion of the effects of Title XX, even though definitive answers to most questions could not be obtained.

Two of the more significant factors affecting the provision of Title XX social services to women and minorities appear to have been eligibility levels and service mix.

o   Universality vs. targeting. There is an essential conflict within Title XX, which is of particular significance to women and minorities, between the law's preference for serving the poor and its goal of making social services more generally available to higher-income individuals and families.

Title XX stipulates that at least half a state's service program (measured in terms of federal expenditures) be devoted to the "categorically eligible" (i.e., recipients of AFDC, SSI, or Medicaid). To the extent that women and minorities are disproportionately represented in these programs, they are more likely to be among the recipients of Title XX-funded social services than are families headed by non-minority group members and males.

With notable exceptions (e.g., programs for the mentally retarded), however, 90 percent of a state's service program prior to Title XX had to be provided to current recipients of public assistance. Title XX not only reduced this proportion to 50 percent, but set the maximum client eligibility level for federal financial participation in social service programs at 115 percent of the state's median income. Although only 17 states have made some or all of their services available to persons with this level of income, only 5 states have restricted client eligibility to families below 70 percent of the median income, levels approximating those of categorically related individuals.

This liberalization came at a time when fiscal resources available for social services were increasingly limited by the expenditure ceiling. In effect, then, the poor must now compete with higher-income families for limited social services. Stated in its most basic terms, movement toward more universal social services, in the absence of an infusion of additional funds, can only be accomplished at the expense of poor families, which are disproportionately headed by women and minorities.

The preceding statement should not be construed as a denial of the validity of other arguments (e.g., destigmatization) for universal social services. It should be pointed out, too, that there are other factors

in Title XX policy and its implementation which may have a particular
effect on women and minorities.

    o  <u>One service vs. another</u>. The second major factor which may
have affected the provision of social services to minorities and women,
positively or negatively, is the mix of services offered. Simply stated,
the choice Title XX agencies make about which <u>services</u> to provide may
result in a de facto choice about which <u>recipients</u> are served. Again,
although national data were not available, the experience of one state
in assessing the proportion of male vs. female recipients of each service
illustrates this point. Table 23 depicts the sex of recipients of various
types of social services in State "A."

It should be obvious from these data that, at least in one state,
the recipients of certain services are predominantly male or female.
Services whose clientele are predominantly female included homemaker/chore,
home management, health related, transportation, family planning, employment and education, assessment, and mobile/congregate meals. Services
which tend to serve a predominantly male clientele included foster care,
chemical dependency, and court-related services. Overall, again in one
state, six out of ten persons classified as "primary recipients" of Title XX
services were females. It should be remembered, however, that there is
substantial concern that the classification of who, in fact, is the
primary recipient for reporting purposes may vary not only from state to
state but from worker to worker.

Comparable data on ethnic or racial backgrounds of the recipients of
each service did not exist. National data comparing the percentage of Title XX

TABLE 23

Allocation of Social Services by Sex in State "A," 1976

| SOCIAL SERVICE | SEX OF RECIPIENT[a] | |
| --- | --- | --- |
| | MALE | FEMALE |
| Chore/Homemaker | 24.3 | 75.4 |
| Foster Care | 57.7 | 41.9 |
| Day Care | 48.6 | 50.9 |
| Home Management | 32.4 | 67.3 |
| Protective Services | 39.5 | 59.7 |
| Health Related | 34.5 | 65.2 |
| Transportation | 21.1 | 78.6 |
| Chemical Dependency | 84.0 | 15.8 |
| Family Planning | 3.8 | 95.9 |
| Sheltered Environment | 50.9 | 48.9 |
| Court Related | 82.2 | 17.8 |
| Employment & Education | 15.6 | 84.1 |
| Assessment | 33.8 | 65.9 |
| Mobile/Cong. Meals | 31.1 | 68.9 |
| Mental Health Related | 42.6 | 57.0 |
| Other | 43.3 | 56.0 |
| Average | 39.7 | 59.9 |

a.  Totals may not add up to 100.0 percent where sex of cases was not identified.

social services provided to AFDC recipients with those provided to income eligibles are available (see table 24). Because a disproportionate number of AFDC recipients are members of minority groups, the choice to offer a mix of services that are utilized by either a disproportionately high or low percentage of AFDC recipients may affect the proportion of social services provided to minorities.

Services utilized by a disproportionately high percentage of AFDC recipients included special services to children and youth, housing improvement, employment services, and day care for children. Conversely, services provided to a greater percentage of income eligibles included home delivered/congregate meals, special services (alcohol and drug), transitional services, and special services to the blind and disabled.

a. <u>Other Factors Favoring Minorities and Women</u>. Although a state's choice of eligibility levels and service mix can have either a positive or negative effect on the provision of services to minorities and women, several aspects of Title XX policy appear to promote a greater opportunity for minorities and women to participate in social services priority-setting. Such factors have at least the potential to increase the responsiveness of service programs. The following elements of Title XX policy are among those most favorable to minorities and women:

o <u>Substate planning</u>. Prior to Title XX, social service programs were required to be statewide. That is, every service provided by a state had to be available throughout the entire state. Title XX permitted states to opt for substate planning and substate variation in the design of a service program. All but 16 states have opted for substate planning.

TABLE 24

Percent of Selected Social Services Received by
Category of Recipient

| | | Category of Recipient | |
| Service | Total Recipients | Percent AFDC | Percent Income Eligibles |
|---|---|---|---|
| Special Services-Child & Youth | 12,764 | 70 | 14 |
| Housing Improvement | 74,164 | 40 | 11 |
| Employment Services | 148,939 | 55 | 24 |
| Day Care-Children | 419,490 | 54 | 30 |
| Legal Services | 102,100 | 53 | 29 |
| Diagnostic & Evaluative | 43,555 | 46 | 25 |
| Foster Care-Children | 208,073 | 44 | 18 |
| Residential Care & Treatment | 76,417 | 40 | 11 |
| Home Management | 155,122 | 40 | 18 |
| Recreational Services | 35,843 | 38 | 17 |
| Health-Related Services | 726,932 | 33 | 10 |
| Emergency Services | 8,290 | 31 | 11 |
| Protective Services-Children | 352,149 | 29 | 6 |
| Family Planning | 258,201 | 25 | 64 |
| Socialization Services | 68,558 | 21 | 40 |
| Adoption | 34,234 | 16 | 38 |
| Special Services-Disabled | 13,620 | 8 | 33 |
| Special Services-Blind | 420 | 8 | 38 |
| Transitional Services | 1,236 | 7 | 50 |
| Special Services-Alcohol & Drug | 11,882 | 7 | 82 |
| Home Delivered/Cong. Meals | 37,894 | 3 | 60 |

Source:  U.S. Department of Health, Education, and Welfare.  "Social Services U.S.A." draft, April-June, 1976, Table 21.

It is, perhaps, ironic that the elimination of the requirement that all services be provided statewide, originally designed to prevent discriminatory service programs, may actually result in services more responsive to the needs of minorities. A primary cause of this enhanced responsiveness is the visibility of substate allocations of Title XX funds, since this visibility has spurred lively discussions about the equity of substate allocations. In addition, because substate areas are granted more discretion under Title XX than under prior titles, they can now design service programs more responsive to the special needs of their residents. Further, to the extent that minorities are unevenly distributed among substate areas, they may have a greater voice in the establishment of social services priorities than they would if those decisions were being made on a statewide basis.

o  Group eligibility. Title XX initially required that eligibility for most social services be determined on an individual basis. It was not until late in 1976 that Title XX was amended by P.L. 94-401 to allow states to once again determine eligibility on a group basis, an option which existed prior to Title XX.

Although it should be obvious that determining eligibility on a group basis will not always favor minorities and women, HEW regulations implementing P.L. 94-401 required that "substantially all" members of groups be members of families with incomes not above 90 percent of the state's median level.

o  Ceiling on Title XX. The $2.5 billion limitation on federal financial participation in Title XX-funded social services may have restricted the growth of social services programs in many jurisdictions. It may certainly be argued, too, that larger social services programs which might result from an increase in the ceiling on Title XX would benefit everyone, including minorities and women. Observations in several of the states most severely constrained by the limitations on federal funds for Title XX social services, however, suggest that one of the unintended consequences of the ceiling may be intertitle transfers (i.e., moving service programs into and out of Title XX, primarily to maximize federal financial participation). The most frequently cited human service programs involved in such transfers are Titles IV-A (AFDC) and XIX (Medicaid). Where the income eligibility criteria for these programs are lower than those of Title XX, families headed by minorities and women may be disproportionately benefited. There is less likelihood that minorities and women would benefit from intertitle transfers involving programs without income restrictions (e.g., Title IV-B of the Social Security Act and the Older Americans Act).

b. <u>Other Factors Not Favoring Minorities and Women</u>. The following elements of Title XX policies may have a negative effect on the provision of social services to women and minorities:

o <u>Ethic of "color blindness."</u> According to personal interviews and the written responses of administrators of provider agencies and senior state administrators, special consideration in Title XX planning is not generally afforded to women and minorities. Respondents frequently commented that services are provided to persons without regard to "race, creed, or color." Senior state administrators generally reflected that they were "color blind" with regard to the formulation of priorities for social services. Similarly, although women's groups were often observed to be interested in such specific services as family planning and day care, such groups were seldom, if ever, active in the overall Title XX planning processes at the state and local level.

The data presented in table 25 generally indicate that special consideration was not given to the needs and service requirements of special groups in Title XX planning. Notable exceptions to this pattern were concerns for the aged, physically disabled, mentally retarded or developmentally disabled, and other recipients of mental health services.

It can be argued that failure to afford women and minorities special consideration in service allocations has neither a favorable nor unfavorable impact; however, such an argument also suggests that any effects (positive or negative) of Title XX on minorities and women would be serendipitous.

o Lack of data. Closely related, perhaps, to the ethic of color blindness is the fairly pervasive lack of data on how Title XX funds are divided among minorities, non-minorities, males, and females. Such data may be collected but are seldom, if ever, analyzed for policy purposes. Thus, even when special efforts are made on behalf of women or minorities, the unavailability of data on service allocation makes it impossible to determine the results of those efforts.

o Media for participation. One of the key factors of Title XX is its provision for public participation in the social services planning process. By and large, however, the portion of the public that has been active and influential in Title XX planning has been representative of neither the consuming or general populations.

Public hearings, display advertisements, and the opportunity to submit comments on a printed CASP plan are media which favor

TABLE 25

Special Consideration Given to the Needs and Service
Requirements of Specific Groups in Title XX Planning

| | Percent of Responses | | | | |
|---|---|---|---|---|---|
| Special Groups | Provider Administrators (n = 174) | | Senior State Admin. (n = 196) | | In-Depth Interviews[a] (n = 322) |
| | Yes | No | Yes | No | |
| Aged | 35.4 (52) | 64.6 (95) | 90.3 (167) | 9.7 (18) | 2.9 |
| Women | 23.9 (34) | 76.1 (108) | 41.1 (72) | 58.9 (103) | 1.6 |
| Minorities: | | | | | |
| a. American Indians or Alaska Natives | 9.8 (10) | 90.2 (92) | 35.0 (48) | 65.0 (89) | 1.6 |
| b. Asians or Pacific Islanders | 9.2 (9) | 90.8 (89) | 26.3 (35) | 73.7 (98) | 1.5 |
| c. Blacks, Not of Hispanic Origin | 22.4 (24) | 77.6 (83) | 43.7 (59) | 56.3 (76) | 2.0 |
| d. Hispanics | 15.7 | 84.3 | 38.1 | 61.9 | 2.0 |
| Residents of Rural Areas | 18.4 (25) | 81.6 (111) | 51.7 (89) | 48.3 (83) | 2.2 |
| Physically Disabled | 18.4 | 81.6 | 51.7 | 48.3 | 2.2 |
| Mentally Retarded or Developmentally Disabled | 31.7 (45) | 68.3 (97) | 93.9 (168) | 6.1 (11) | n.a. |
| Other Recipients of Mental Health Services | 33.6 (47) | 66.4 (93) | 76.6 (134) | 23.4 (41) | n.a. |

Note: "n.a." denotes data not available.

a. Average assessment based on a scale from 1 (indicating little or no special consideration) to 5 (indicating extensive consideration given to the needs and service requirements of special groups).

participation by organized and articulate segments of the public (e.g., government agencies and other providers of social services).

o <u>Contracting procedures</u>. Women and minorities are providers, as well as consumers, of social services. HEW regulations implementing Title XX imposed the first meaningful national requirements on state and local contracting for social services. Until the regulations were recently amended, for example, individual contracts were required for each vendor, regardless of the number of persons employed.

Although close examination of state contracting and reporting procedures was beyond the scope of the Institute's study, those procedures were frequently cited as being extremely complex and often undocumented. Also frequently heard were complaints by potential providers about the "seed money" required to begin service provision and the lag in reimbursement which often necessitated that providers finance six months' expenditures before reimbursement was received from the state or local Title XX agency. Such constraints were often cited by respondents as being barriers to the provision of service by minority contractors.

o <u>Indian sovereignty</u>. A somewhat anomalous development in Title XX implementation has been how this legislation has been intertwined in the broader issue of Indian sovereignty. Oversimplified, the Indian nations contend that they are, in fact, independent nations which should receive Title XX and other funds directly from the federal government rather than through a single state agency or other intermediary.

c. <u>Net Effect of Title XX on Minorities and Women</u>. Data confirming the effects of any one factor of Title XX policy on minorities and women are limited. Summary data on the net effect of all factors, including those which have not been discussed here, are somewhat more available.

Table 26 suggests, based on very limited observations, that black, Spanish-surnamed, and other non-white populations tend to receive social services to a larger degree than their proportion of the population generally eligible for Title XX services in the selected states.

As table 27 indicates, although comparable data based on income by sex in each state are not presented, female recipients of Title XX-funded social services comprise from one-half to more than two-thirds of the service population in the states for which data were available.

2. Effects on the Aging

To assess the impact of Title XX on the aging two questions will be addressed:

> o What factors in Title XX policy favor or limit the provision of services to older people?
>
> o What effects, if any, has state implementation of Title XX had on the allocation of services to older people?

a. Relevant Features of Title XX. In its assessment of Title XX's implementation, The Urban Institute identified the major factors which could be expected to have an effect, positive or negative, on the allocation of resources to the aging. The major factors which could be expected to increase the portion of funds supporting social services to older persons included:

> o Mandated services for SSI recipients. Each state was required to include in its Comprehensive Annual Services Program (CASP) plan at least three services for recipients of Supplemental Security Income (SSI). Although the majority of SSI recipients are disabled and blind persons rather than older persons receiving public assistance, these

TABLE 26

Allocation of Social Services by Race in Selected
States, 1974-1976

| | Percent of Eligible Population[a] | Percent of Total Services | | |
| --- | --- | --- | --- | --- |
| | | 1974 | 1975 | 1976 |
| State "C" | | | | |
| White | 98.6 | n.a. | 90.9 | 88.7 |
| Black | 1.2 | n.a. | 6.3 | 7.3 |
| Spanish-Surnamed | 0.2 | n.a. | 0.7 | 0.9 |
| State "D" | | | | |
| White | 98.4 | 88.7 | 88.5 | 91.3 |
| Black | 1.1 | 7.3 | 6.4 | 4.7 |
| Spanish-Surnamed | 0.5 | 1.9 | 1.7 | 1.6 |
| Other | -- | 2.1 | 3.4 | 2.3 |
| State "E" | | | | |
| White | 98.4 | 93.8 | 93.8 | 94.1 |
| Black | 1.1 | 5.1 | 5.2 | 5.0 |
| Spanish-Surnamed | 0.5 | 0.2 | 0.4 | 0.5 |
| Other | -- | 0.9 | 0.6 | 0.4 |
| State "F" | | | | |
| White | 72.7 | n.a. | n.a. | 46.6 |
| Black | 25.4 | n.a. | n.a. | 51.8 |
| Other | 1.9 | n.a. | n.a. | 1.6 |

a. Based on the racial composition of the population below the income level most closely approximating Title XX eligibility levels in each state.

TABLE 27

Allocation of Social Services by Sex in
Selected States, 1974-1977

| | Percent of Total Services | | | |
|---|---|---|---|---|
| | 1974 | 1975 | 1976 | 1977 |
| State "G" | | | | |
| Male | n.a. | n.a. | 39.9 | 36.7 |
| Female | n.a. | n.a. | 60.1 | 63.3 |
| State "H" | | | | |
| Male | n.a. | n.a. | 41.4 | n.a. |
| Female | n.a. | n.a. | 58.6 | n.a. |
| State "I" | | | | |
| Male | 49.6 | 49.5 | n.a. | n.a. |
| Female | 50.4 | 50.5 | n.a. | n.a. |
| State "J" | | | | |
| Male | 30.3 | 32.9 | 37.0 | n.a. |
| Female | 69.7 | 67.1 | 53.0 | n.a. |
| State "K" | | | | |
| Male | n.a. | n.a. | 32.8 | n.a. |
| Female | n.a. | n.a. | 67.2 | n.a. |

populations were the only groups singled out by the federal government for program priority under Title XX.

o <u>Sensitive population and visible services</u>. It was anticipated that by broadening the base of public participation in social services priority-setting, services for the aging would tend to benefit, since concern and sensitivity about the service needs of older persons were increasing. Further, the services provided to older persons (e.g., homemaker services) tended to be more visible and tangible than services often provided to other groups (e.g., counseling).

o <u>Organization</u>. Title XX substituted an open planning process for the state-federal accountability which characterized prior legislation. Accountability under Title XX was to a state's citizenry and elected leadership, rather than to the federal government. It was anticipated that groups which were organized and articulate would benefit more in such an environment than groups which lacked comparable staff or advocacy mechanisms. Older persons had an existing network of state and area agencies on aging which were capable of playing a significant role in Title XX decision-making.

Factors which were identified as tending to restrict or reduce the proportion of Title XX funds devoted to services for older person included:

o <u>Title XX is a "zero-sum game."</u> As noted above, federal funds for social services have been limited since 1972. Expanded programs for the aging, in view of the ceiling, were often seen as coming at the expense of services to other populations (e.g., children and youth).

o <u>Availability of non-Title XX funds</u>. A not uncommon attitude detected by Institute interviewers was that because older persons had access to federal funding sources other than Title XX (most frequently mentioned were appropriations for service programs under the Older Americans Act), funds to expand programs for the aging should be drawn from those other sources, rather than from Title XX.

o <u>Setting for publicly funded social services</u>.  It was anticipated that, to some extent, the setting for publicly funded social services (e.g., local welfare offices) would deter older persons from seeking or receiving social services.  Not only is accepting "welfare" a blow to the pride of many older persons, but the aging (unlike families with children) rarely come into contact with local welfare offices, at least since implementation of SSI.

b.  <u>Pattern of Services to the Elderly</u>.  Perhaps the most appropriate method to measure the effect of Title XX on the elderly is to examine the delivery pattern of services to the aged.  When Title XX was established, a set of Social Services Reporting Requirements (SSRR) was also initiated. SSRR data are beginning to provide a picture of the pattern of service delivery across the nation.

SSRR data, however, do have certain limitations.  The limitation that most significantly hinders examination of the pattern of service delivery to the elderly is that services are not reported by age of recipient, but by the recipient's eligibility category.  Consequently, no national mechanism exists to determine how many elderly persons are actually receiving social services.  Nevertheless, approximations can be made on a number of bases:

o <u>A comparison with general population</u>.  The group clearly defined as elderly in the Title XX reporting format is the "SSI-aged" category.  The proportion of SSI aged recipients to all Title XX recipients as compared to the proportion of elderly recipients (defined here as aged 62

and above) to the total population of each state is shown in table 28.
Nationwide, the elderly comprise 12 percent of the total population,
while 7.8 percent of Title XX services go to SSI aged recipients.  This
is not an accurate measure of services to the aged, however, since many
recipients in the "income eligible," "without regard to income," and
"medical assistance" categories may very well be elderly.

o  Comparison with categorically related population.  Another
possible way to measure services provided to the elderly would be to
compare the percentage of the SSI aged receiving services to the total
categorically related (AFDC, SSI, MA) population receiving services.  This
comparison is presented in table 29.

Although SSI aged comprise 7.6 percent of the total categorically
related population, they receive 7.8 percent of the services.  In view of
the fact that the income eligible categories are included in the Title XX
services population, the SSI aged generally appear to be receiving a proportion of services relative to their size.  This varies, of course, by
state.  Unfortunately, this method of comparison, too, presents a limited
picture of services to the aged.

o  Direct comparison.  In an attempt to make a more direct
comparison, The Urban Institute collected detailed data on services to the
elderly in five study states (Iowa, Michigan, New York, North Carolina,
and Oregon).  These data are age-specific and include all eligibility
categories.  While the data are not consistent across jurisdictions, some
general indications of the level of services to the elderly can be
ascertained from them (see table 30).

In general, it appears that the elderly comprise either a
comparable or larger portion of the services population than of the general

TABLE 28

Percent of Title XX Services to SSI Aged
Compared to Percent of Total Population
62 Years and Over

| State | Percent of Total Population 62 Years & Over[a] | SSI Aged as Percent of Recipients of Title XX Services[b] |
|-------|------------------------------------------------|------------------------------------------------------------|
| Alabama | 12.0 | 9.1 |
| Alaska | 3.2 | 9.3 |
| Arizona | 11.5 | 0.5 |
| Arkansas | 15.3 | 12.1 |
| California | 11.2 | 13.0 |
| Colorado | 10.6 | 9.6 |
| Connecticut | 11.9 | 1.4 |
| Delaware | 10.1 | 4.2 |
| District of Columbia | 11.9 | 4.3 |
| Florida | 17.7 | 5.1 |
| Georgia | 10.2 | 7.3 |
| Hawaii | 7.4 | 6.3 |
| Idaho | 11.9 | 4.8 |
| Illinois | 12.3 | 4.2 |
| Indiana | 11.8 | 1.0 |
| Iowa | 15.0 | 7.6 |
| Kansas | 14.5 | 3.0 |
| Kentucky | 13.0 | 6.5 |
| Louisiana | 10.7 | 9.1 |
| Maine | 14.2 | 4.3 |
| Maryland | 9.7 | 10.8 |
| Massachusetts | 13.7 | 12.9 |
| Michigan | 10.6 | 6.6 |
| Minnesota | 13.1 | 3.1 |
| Mississippi | 12.6 | 9.3 |
| Missouri | 14.8 | 13.4 |
| Montana | 12.2 | 5.2 |
| Nebraska | 15.0 | 8.9 |
| Nevada | 8.4 | 11.6 |
| New Hampshire | 13.1 | 4.4 |
| New Jersey | 12.2 | 3.1 |
| New Mexico | 8.9 | 11.5 |
| New York | 13.4 | 6.7 |
| North Carolina | 10.4 | 9.7 |
| North Dakota | 13.3 | 6.2 |
| Ohio | 11.7 | 7.0 |
| Oklahoma | 14.5 | 9.7 |
| Oregon | 13.4 | 10.8 |
| Pennsylvania | 13.5 | 6.6 |
| Rhode Island | 13.6 | 6.1 |
| South Carolina | 9.4 | 10.2 |
| South Dakota | 14.6 | 5.0 |
| Tennessee | 12.3 | 5.2 |
| Texas | 11.1 | 12.4 |
| Utah | 9.2 | 5.8 |
| Vermont | 13.1 | 5.0 |
| Virginia | 10.0 | 5.8 |
| Washington | 11.7 | 5.9 |
| West Virginia | 14.0 | 13.7 |
| Wisconsin | 13.2 | 1.6 |
| Wyoming | 11.4 | 2.8 |
| Average | 12.1 | 7.8 |

a. Based on figures in table 62, "General Population Characteristics, U.S. Summary," 1970 Census of Population (PC (1)-B-1).
b. Based on data from tables 1 and 3, "Social Services, U.S.A.," April-June, 1976. Data include Title IV-B and IV-C Recipients "continued from last period" and "initiated this period."

TABLE 29

## Percent of Title XX Services to SSI Aged Compared to Percent of Total Categorically Related Population

| State | SSI Aged As Percent of Total Categorical Population (AFDC, SSI, M.A.)[a] | Percent of all Title XX Services Received by SSI Aged[b] |
|---|---|---|
| Alabama | 15.7 | 9.1 |
| Alaska | 6.5 | 9.3 |
| Arizona | 14.2 | 0.5 |
| Arkansas | 11.8 | 12.1 |
| California | 5.6 | 13.0 |
| Colorado | 7.8 | 9.6 |
| Connecticut | 2.7 | 1.4 |
| Delaware | 4.1 | 4.2 |
| District of Columbia | 2.1 | 4.3 |
| Florida | 12.0 | 5.1 |
| Georgia | 9.9 | 7.3 |
| Hawaii | 3.5 | 6.3 |
| Idaho | 7.0 | 4.8 |
| Illinois | 2.5 | 4.2 |
| Indiana | 5.5 | 1.0 |
| Iowa | 7.5 | 7.6 |
| Kansas | 5.6 | 3.0 |
| Kentucky | 10.1 | 6.5 |
| Louisiana | 15.0 | 9.1 |
| Maine | 6.3 | 4.3 |
| Maryland | 0.7 | 10.8 |
| Massachusetts | 5.6 | 12.9 |
| Michigan | 3.0 | 6.6 |
| Minnesota | 4.9 | 3.1 |
| Mississippi | 14.6 | 9.3 |
| Missouri | 10.1 | 13.4 |
| Montana | 5.6 | 5.2 |
| Nebraska | 7.4 | 8.9 |
| Nevada | 8.8 | 11.6 |
| New Hampshire | 4.2 | 4.4 |
| New Jersey | 3.5 | 3.1 |
| New Mexico | 7.6 | 11.5 |
| New York | 3.8 | 6.7 |
| North Carolina | 14.1 | 9.7 |
| North Dakota | 10.6 | 6.2 |
| Ohio | 4.0 | 7.0 |
| Oklahoma | 13.2 | 9.7 |
| Oregon | 4.2 | 10.8 |
| Pennsylvania | 2.8 | 6.6 |
| Rhode Island | 3.9 | 6.1 |
| South Carolina | 11.1 | 10.2 |
| South Dakota | 9.2 | 5.0 |
| Tennessee | 13.3 | 5.2 |
| Texas | 14.6 | 12.4 |
| Utah | 3.4 | 5.8 |
| Vermont | 6.2 | 5.0 |
| Virginia | 7.2 | 5.8 |
| Washington | 4.4 | 5.9 |
| West Virginia | 8.7 | 13.7 |
| Wisconsin | 6.6 | 1.6 |
| Wyoming | 5.0 | 2.8 |
| Average | 7.6 | 7.8 |

a. Based on figures in "Statistical Abstracts," 1975, Table 490, "Public Assistance Recipients of Money Payments, States and Other Areas: 1974," and "Numbers of Recipients and Amounts of Payments Under Medicaid, (FY) 1974," (Advance Copy), HEW, Social and Rehabilitation Service.
b. Based on data from tables 1 and 3, "Social Services, U.S.A.," April-June, 1976. Data include Title IV-B and IV-C Recipients "continued from last period" and "initiated this period."

TABLE 30

Five-State Comparison of Percent of Services Received
by the Elderly Contrasted with Percent of Older Persons
in General Population

| States | Percent of Elderly in Services Population | Percent of Service Expenditures on Elderly | Percent of Elderly in Total State Population |
|--------|-------------------------------------------|--------------------------------------------|----------------------------------------------|
| M | 26.7 | n.a. | 16.9 |
| N | 12.5 | 20.2 | 12.3 |
| O | n.a. | 16.4 | 15.5 |
| P | 19.3 | 21.0 | 12.1 |
| Q | 10.7 | 15.8 | 15.4 |

a.  Percentages are from U.S. Bureau of the Census, General Population
Characteristics, PC(2)-B39 (1969), table 21.

population and are receiving either a comparable or larger proportion of Title XX service expenditures than would be suggested by their proportion of the state's population.

Although the number of observations are limited and the five study states are not representative, in a statistical sense, of the entire nation, this finding is significant since the major purpose of intervention in Title XX by state and area agencies on Aging has been to secure a "fair share" of expenditures under that program. These limited data suggest that this goal has been accomplished.

D.  CHANGES IN ALLOCATION OF RESOURCES AMONG SUBSTATE AREAS

Given the general dearth of credible cost-benefit data or knowledge about social services program effectiveness (i.e., "what works"), it is difficult to respond to the demands of competing groups on any basis other than a political one. Since it is virtually impossible, then, to argue that one pattern of allocation is demonstrably better than another, and given the inherent complexity of social services, demands for equity tend to be very important in the Title XX decision-making process. Notions of equity generally translate into a fair share for alternative eligible population groups (e.g., the aging), a balanced program of alternative social services (e.g., day care vs. homemaker/chore), and a reasonably equitable distribution of resources to substate areas (e.g., City X, County Y, or upstate).

The data in table 31 indicate that 16 states utilized the state as a whole as the geographic base for their CASP plans, while the remaining jurisdictions utilized other substate areas (e.g., combinations of cities and counties, groups of jurisdictions, planning districts, the geographic areas of other human service programs, or other regions). It is

## TABLE 31

### Extent of Substate Planning for Title XX

| State/Region | Geographic Base for CASP[a] | Extent of Substate Planning[b][c] | State or Local Control Enhanced[b] | Criteria for Sub-State Allocation[b] |
|---|---|---|---|---|
| **I. Boston** | | | | |
| Connecticut | State | 4 | No Change | Caseload, Needs |
| Maine | State | 1 | No Change | N.A. |
| Massachusetts | Substate | 1 | No Change | N.A. |
| New Hampshire | State | 4 | No Change | N.A. |
| Rhode Island | State | 1 | No Change | N.A. |
| Vermont | State | 1 | No Change | N.A. |
| **II. New York** | | | | |
| New Jersey | State | 3 | Local | Experience, Population |
| New York | County | 5 | State | Experience, Population |
| **III. Philadelphia** | | | | |
| District of Columbia | Substate | N.A. | N.A. | N.A. |
| Delaware | State | 1 | Local | Needs |
| Maryland | County | N.A. | N.A. | N.A. |
| Pennsylvania | Substate | 1 | No Change | N.A. |
| Virginia | Substate | 5 | Local | Population, Experience |
| West Virginia | Substate | 3 | Local | Caseload, Population |
| **IV. Atlanta** | | | | |
| Alabama | County | 2 | No Change | N.A. |
| Florida | Substate | 3 | No Change | N.A. |
| Georgia | Substate | 1 | No Change | N.A. |
| Kentucky | Substate | 4 | No Change | N.A. |
| Mississippi | County | 1 | State | Match |
| North Carolina | County | 4 | No Change | Poor Population |
| South Carolina | Substate | 4 | State | N.A. |
| Tennessee | Substate | 4 | No Change | Population, Caseload |
| **V. Chicago** | | | | |
| Illinois | State | 1 | State | N.A. |
| Indiana | County | 1 | State | N.A. |
| Michigan | State | 1 | State | Experience, Caseload, Population |
| Minnesota | Substate | 5 | State | Experience, Population, Caseload, Econ. Factors |
| Ohio | County | N.A. | N.A. | N.A. |
| Wisconsin | Substate | N.A. | N.A. | N.A. |
| **VI. Dallas** | | | | |
| Arkansas | Substate | 4 | State | N.A. |
| Louisiana | County | 4 | State | Need, Requests, Match |
| New Mexico | Substate | 3 | Local | Low Income Population |
| Oklahoma | State | 3 | Local | N.A. |
| Texas | State | 3 | Local | Need, Match, Priorities, Demographics |
| **VII. Kansas City** | | | | |
| Iowa | Substate | 3 | Local | Experience, Population |
| Kansas | State | N.A. | N.A. | N.A. |
| Missouri | Substate | 2 | Local | N.A. |
| Nebraska | State | 4 | Local | Needs, Population |
| **VIII. Denver** | | | | |
| Colorado | County | 3 | No Change | Experience |
| Montana | Substate | 1 | No Change | N.A. |
| North Dakota | County | 5 | Local | Experience, Service Patterns |
| South Dakota | Substate | 1 | State | N.A. |
| Utah | Substate | 4 | State | Match, Needs |
| Wyoming | State | 2 | Local | N.A. |
| **IX. San Francisco** | | | | |
| Arizona | Substate | 4 | Local | Poor, Aged, Caseload |
| California | County | 2 | State | Experience |
| Hawaii | County | 3 | State | N.A. |
| Nevada | Substate | 4 | State | N.A. |
| **X. Seattle** | | | | |
| Alaska | State | 3 | Local | Population, Needs, Costs |
| Idaho | Substate | 5 | State | Requests, Legis. Budget |
| Oregon | State | 1 | No Change | Experience |
| Washington | Substate | 5 | State | Special Population, Density, Needs |

a. ASPE Technical Notes.
b. Urban Institute research in eight states supplemented by HEW Regional Office perceptions.
c. Extent of substate planning ranges from 1 (denoting little or none) to 5 (indicating extensive). "N.A." denotes data not available.

interesting to note in passing that although a large number of states
in which Title XX is administered directly by the state have utilized
substate areas as the geographic base for their CASPs, only three
locally administered jurisdictions utilize the state as a whole as
the basis for their CASPs. This generally reflects strong state control
over local programs, restriction of the service program to a few core
services available statewide, use of state expenditures to equalize
programs statewide, or a desire for administrative simplicity.

Regional office observers and respondents in the eight states in
which the Institute conducted an in-depth study were asked to describe
the extent of substate planning in their respective jurisdictions.
Possible responses ranged from 1, indicating little or none, to 5,
denoting extensive. The responses and observations indicated that
jurisdictions with more than moderate substate planning were counter-
balanced by an equal number of jurisdictions with less than moderate
substate planning (14 jurisdictions each). Further, there appeared to
be no clear correlation between selection of geographic base and the
extent of substate planning. That is, jurisdictions opting for substate
bases for their CASP plans were neither more nor less likely to have
more than moderate substate planning than were jurisdictions opting
for statewide bases.

1.  Enhancement of Local Control

The first year's evaluation of the implementation of Title XX
indicated that respondents and observers generally felt that local control had been enhanced as a result of Title XX. In assessing these data,
the Institute made the following observations:

o    The predecessor legislation to Title XX (i.e., Titles IV-A
and VI) also granted authority to states; thus, the authority of states
vis-a-vis local government was not enhanced by Title XX.

o    Even where an expanded role for local governments and social
service directors, boards, and staffs is observed or expected as a result
of Title XX, it frequently is only in the form of input into decisions
which are made at the state level.

o    Responses that indicate that the local role in social
services organization and management has been strengthened by Title XX
do not indicate that it is the local level of government which is in
control of social services.

o    Even where strengthened local influence in the organization
and management of social services was reported, it was often the regional,
district, or area offices of the state agency which were perceived as
having played the larger role.

o    On a national level, public interest groups such as the
National Association of Counties were active in the passage of Title XX
and made a substantial effort to keep their membership informed of their
potential role in Title XX.

2.    Absence of Criteria for Substate Allocation

Observers and respondents in each state were asked what criteria were
utilized to allocate Title XX funds to substate areas.  The most frequent
response was, "I don't know."  Even in the eight states studied in-depth,
only a relatively small proportion of all respondents were aware of the
criteria employed in substate allocation.

A separate mailout instrument was completed by 197 senior state
administrators in 13 states.  Their responses to the question, "Which of

the following statements describe the criteria which are used to allocate funds to substate areas?" are set forth in table 32.

These data indicate that the primary criteria upon which substate allocations are based are the availability of non-federal (i.e., matching) funds, the pre-Title XX allocation of services, analysis of caseload data and other (including political) criteria. Table 33 shows the relative weights attached to primary criteria in the eight states studied in-depth.

It is interesting to note that in only a few instances do states base their substate allocations of Title XX funds on a single criterion. No state allocates funds solely on the basis of population, the only criterion used by the federal government to allocate funds to states. It is important to understand, then, how these criteria tend to work in combination with one another.

3. Policy Implications

a. Title XX funds are allocated within a state even in the absence of an explicit allocation formula. It may appear from the discussion above that the only states which allocate funds to substate areas are those with well-defined allocation formulae. However, this is not true. The presence or absence of allocation formulae do affect the method by which allocations are made and the visibility of the allocation processes. In the absence of explicit criteria for substate allocation, allocations are made (if only incrementally) via the deployment of staff, location of service facilities, awarding of service contracts, and the like.

b. The planned allocation of funds may differ greatly from the actual use of funds. The Institute's field work and an independent review by the Administration for Public Services of CASP/SSRR data indicate that actual

TABLE 32

Criteria for Substate Allocation

| Criteria | Yes | | No | |
|---|---|---|---|---|
| | # | % | # | % |
| Availability of non-federal (i.e., matching) funds | 117 | 70.0 | 50 | 30.0 |
| Pre-Title XX allocation of services | 119 | 72.1 | 46 | 27.9 |
| Analysis of caseload data | 101 | 62.3 | 61 | 37.7 |
| Known formula based primarily on general population | 52 | 34.4 | 101 | 65.6 |
| Known formula based primarily on the population believed to be eligible for Title XX services | 65 | 41.4 | 92 | 58.6 |
| Results of needs assessment(s) | 67 | 42.4 | 91 | 57.6 |
| Availability of service providers | 91 | 44.2 | 72 | 55.8 |
| Other (including political) criteria | 69 | 63.9 | 39 | 36.1 |

## TABLE 33

### Basis for Substate Allocation in Eight States

| STATE | FORMULA Yes/No | Year Estab. | BASIS FOR ALLOCATION (Weight) | REALLOCATION[a] |
|---|---|---|---|---|
| Arizona | yes | 1977 | Planning Districts<br>o AFDC Caseload (25%)<br>o SSI Caseload (25%)<br>o Families below Median Income (25%)<br>o Families in Poverty Headed by Persons 65 Years and Older (25%) | no |
|  | yes | 1977 | Indian Reservations<br>o Population (100%) | no |
| California | yes | 1977 | Highest Expenditures Past Three Years plus 6% Cost of Living | yes |
| Iowa |  |  |  |  |
|  | no | -- | Direct Service Programs<br>o Past Experience (100%) | no |
|  | no | no | Statewide Purchase of Service:<br>o Past Experience (100%) | no |
|  | yes | 1977 | Local Purchase of Service<br>o Past Experience (90%)<br>o Population (10%) | yes |
| Michigan |  |  |  |  |
|  | yes | 1977 | Donated Funds<br>o AFDC, SSI & Food Stamp Caseload (57%)<br>o Population (29%)<br>o Past Experience (14%) | yes |
|  | no | -- | All Other Past Experience | yes |
| New York | yes | 1972 | <br>o Population (50%)<br>o FY 1972 Expenditures (50%) | yes |
| North Carolina |  |  |  |  |
|  | yes | 1977 | FY 1978<br>o Past Experience (80%)<br>o AFDC, SSI, and Medicaid Caseloads (20%) | yes |
|  | yes | 1977 | FY 1979<br>o Past Experience (50%)<br>o AFDC, SSI, and Medicaid Caseloads (50%) | yes |
|  | yes | 1977 | FY 1980<br>o AFDC, SSI, and Medicaid Caseloads (100%) | yes |
| Oregon | no | -- | Past Experience | no |
| Texas | no | -- | Negotiated on the Basis of<br>o Need<br>o Availability of Match<br>o DPW and Legislative Priorities | yes |

a. "Reallocation" is the process by which states redistribute funds from substate areas spending less than their allocation to areas which are spending, or would like to spend, in excess of their initial allocation.

performance may be greatly different from planned performance. Many states, in addition to facing obvious problems related to administering a large network of organizations, lack mechanisms for timely feedback on actual performance (i.e., the intelligence data upon which to base corrective actions). To a large extent, too, social services priorities are determined by individual caseworkers on a case-by-case basis.

c. Even where explicit criteria for substate allocation are utilized, they do not generally extend over the entire Title XX program. Significant items may be excluded from the purview of substate allocation processes. Most frequently excluded are state agency central administrative expenses, direct service programs, purchases of service with statewide providers or other state agencies, and, more recently, the additional funds authorized for day care under P.L. 94-401.

d. Policies of reallocation may be as important as the initial allocation. It is not uncommon for an explicit substate allocation policy to exist in the absence of any articulated method of reallocation. Concerns over reallocation (redistribution of unspent funds from one substate area to another) have surfaced not only in states which have reached their ceiling, but in states below their ceiling where a particular substate area may wish to expand the proportion of funds it receives beyond its "fair share."

e. The geographic basis selected for CASP planning may influence the nature of social services offered. One effect of the abolition of "state-wideness" requirements in several of the states in which the Institute conducted its study has been the development of an increasingly diverse mix of social service programs. This has been particularly true in states which had been below their ceiling. Several of these services (e.g., sheltered workshops and programs for specialized populations) could not have been offered without engaging in a substantial ruse were the geographic basis for CASP planning the state as a whole.

f. <u>Other effects</u>. A clear picture of the substate beneficiary pattern of state practice does not emerge from the jurisdictions in which the Institute has conducted in-depth research. In several states, reallocation formulae adversely affect the more urban jurisdictions and benefit the more rural. In others, the most apparent characteristic of the counties hurt by the allocation and reallocation formulae is that they had been more aggressive in expanding their service programs prior to Title XX.

One interesting feature of the states studied, however, is that the areas in which the state capitals are located would appear to be placed at an inordinate disadvantage by changes in allocation formulae. The disproportionately large social services programs that now exist in state capital areas may have resulted from the location of a large number of state institutions (e.g., corrections, mental health, and nursing facilities) and articulate program advocates and service providers within their bounds. Changes in allocations may tend to decrease the size of social services programs in these areas.

## E. PURCHASE OF SERVICE

Another major area of concern regarding the allocation of resources is the distribution between purchased services and services provided directly by the state or county social service agency. Purchase of service is now the predominant mode of service delivery under Title XX. It has become a major industry amounting to well over $1 billion annually.

The use of purchase of service by state and local agencies as an alternate service delivery method by state and local agencies did not develop until the late 1960s. Its increased usage, then, is due in large measure to the effects of the passage of the 1967 Amendments to the Social Security Act, which authorized states to purchase services from both public and private agencies. A national survey revealed that by 1971 purchased services constituted 25 percent of service expenditures under the legislation that preceded Title XX. Under the open-ended federal social services appropriation, the purchase of social services from other providers, rather than direct provision by the state agency, expanded rapidly, even though there was some slowing down after 1972 when Congress imposed the $2.5 billion limit on federal social services expenditures.

1. Degree of Change in the Direct vs. Purchase Ratio

It was estimated that 53 percent of all expenditures for social services delivered in the second year of Title XX funding would be purchased from public and private providers, rather than delivered directly by the single state agency.

If national data were available which excluded state direct administrative costs (although the actual amount of provider overhead is not known), it is quite likely that more than two-thirds of all Title XX-funded services are provided by agencies other than state or local service departments.

It was anticipated by respondents that there will continue to be a moderate increase in the percentage of Title XX-funded services purchased from other providers or agencies as opposed to those provided directly by the single state agency.

Although data are not totally comparable because not all states purchase from both public and private providers, the percentage of expenditures appears divided about evenly between those services purchased from public sources and those purchased from private providers. Table 34 illustrates on a state-by-state basis the projections made by respondents in each of the federal regional

TABLE 34

Estimated Percentage of Title XX Expenditures
Devoted to Purchase of Service in Each State

| | PERCENT OF TOTAL EXPENDITURES IN 1976 | | | | PERCENT OF TOTAL EXPENDITURES IN 1977 | | | |
|---|---|---|---|---|---|---|---|---|
| State/Region | Other State Agencies | Non-state Public Agencies | Private Agencies | Total | Other State Agencies | Non-state Public Agencies | Private Agencies | Total |
| **I. Boston** | | | | | | | | |
| Connecticut | 76 | 4 | 8 | 88 | 65 | 8 | 15 | 88 |
| Maine | 3 | 0 | 69 | 72 | 3 | 0 | 70 | 73 |
| Massachusetts | 27 | 0 | 14 | 41 | 35 | 0 | 15 | 50 |
| New Hampshire | 5 | 5 | 55 | 65 | 5 | 5 | 55 | 65 |
| Rhode Island | 21 | 0 | 20 | 41 | 14 | 0 | 21 | 35 |
| Vermont | 10 | 10 | 40 | 60 | 10 | 10 | 40 | 60 |
| **II. New York** | | | | | | | | |
| New Jersey | 1 | 3 | 42 | 45 | 1 | 3 | 40 | 43 |
| New York | 1 | 4 | 46 | 51 | 1 | 4 | 44 | 49 |
| **III. Philadelphia** | | | | | | | | |
| District of Columbia | 0 | 5 | 35 | 40 | | | | |
| Delaware[a] | 0 | 26 | 40 | 66 | 0 | 26 | 40 | 66 |
| Maryland | 15 | 7 | 4 | 26 | 15 | 5 | 3 | 23 |
| Pennsylvania[a] | 26 | 22 | 31 | 79 | 28 | 22 | 31 | 79 |
| Virginia | 5 | 10 | 20 | 35 | 3 | 12 | 25 | 40 |
| West Virginia | 18 | 5 | 10 | 33 | 20 | 5 | 15 | 40 |
| **IV. Atlanta** | | | | | | | | |
| Alabama | 22 | 23 | 0 | 45 | 22 | 23 | 0 | 45 |
| Florida | 2 | 14 | 27 | 43 | 2 | 14 | 27 | 43 |
| Georgia | 5 | 40 | 0 | 45 | 5 | 40 | | 45 |
| Kentucky | 1 | 33 | 10 | 44 | 1 | 33 | 10 | 44 |
| Mississippi[a] | 32 | 8 | 17 | 57 | 36 | 9 | 12 | 57 |
| North Carolina | 15 | 5 | 3 | 23 | | | | |
| South Carolina | 37 | 10 | 7 | 59 | 37 | 10 | 7 | 54 |
| Tennessee | 9 | 15 | 36 | 60 | 9 | 15 | 36 | 60 |
| **V. Chicago** | | | | | | | | |
| Illinois | | 70 | 20 | 90 | | 70 | 20 | 90 |
| Indiana | 35 | 0 | 25 | 60 | | | | |
| Michigan | | | | 43 | 5 | 0 | | 34 |
| Minnesota | | | | 57 | | | 20 | 41 |
| Ohio | | | | | | 0 | | 61 |
| Wisconsin | 0 | | 50 | 50 | 0 | | 45 | 45 |

## TABLE 34 (CONTINUED)

| State/Region | PERCENT OF TOTAL EXPENDITURES IN 1976 | | | | PERCENT OF TOTAL EXPENDITURES IN 1977 | | | |
|---|---|---|---|---|---|---|---|---|
| | Other State Agencies | Non-State Public Agencies | Private Agencies | Total | Other State Agencies | Non-State Public Agencies | Private Agencies | Total |
| **VI. Dallas** | | | | | | | | |
| Arkansas | 20 | 0 | 68 | 88 | 18 | 0 | 70 | 88 |
| Louisiana | 14 | 3 | 25 | 42 | 18 | 3 | 29 | 50 |
| New Mexico | 20 | 10 | 15 | 45 | 25 | 12 | 20 | 57 |
| Oklahoma | | | | | | | | |
| Texas | 9 | 7 | 38 | 54 | 5 | 5 | 50 | 60 |
| **VII. Kansas City** | | | | | | | | |
| Iowa | 18 | 18 | 8 | 44 | | | | 51 |
| Kansas | 0 | 38 | 9 | 47 | | | | 61 |
| Missouri | 17 | 12 | 23 | 52 | 26 | 16 | 27 | 69 |
| Nebraska | 0 | 50 | 9 | 59 | 0 | 38 | 25 | 63 |
| **VIII. Denver** | | | | | | | | |
| Colorado | 15 | 0 | 15 | 30 | 15 | 0 | 15 | 30 |
| Montana | 3 | 0 | 50 | 53 | 3 | 0 | 57 | 60 |
| North Dakota | 0 | 0 | 9 | 9 | | | | |
| South Dakota | 10 | 20 | 20 | 50 | 10 | 20 | 30 | 60 |
| Utah | 43 | 14 | 28 | 85 | 42 | 18 | 27 | 87 |
| Wyoming | 2 | 2 | 51 | 55 | 0 | 2 | 55 | 57 |
| **IX. San Francisco** | | | | | | | | |
| Arizona | | | | | 7 | 15 | 42 | 64 |
| California | 20 | 2 | 17 | 39 | 15 | 2 | 20 | 37 |
| Hawaii | | | | 60 | | | | 60 |
| Nevada | 27 | 3 | 0 | 30 | 27 | 3 | 0 | 30 |
| **X. Seattle** | | | | | | | | |
| Alaska | | | 38 | 38 | | | 40 | 40 |
| Idaho | 5 | 2 | 15 | 22 | 5 | 2 | 15 | 22 |
| Oregon | | | 41 | 41 | | | 40 | 40 |
| Washington | | | | | | | | |
| **MEAN:** | 19 | 14 | 29 | 49 | 20 | 14 | 32 | 53 |

Source:  The Urban Institute Title XX Study:  HEW Regional Office Survey

Note:  Blank observations indicate no response from regional offices

a.  Percentages adjusted to reflect proportion of total service delivery

offices of anticipated expenditures for purchase of Title XX-funded
services during both the first and second year of Title XX's implementation. All states purchase some services, and it is estimated that
23 states will have purchased 50 percent or more of their Title XX
services during the second year.

2.  Criteria for Purchase vs. Direct Decisions

Although many states have written policies governing the purchase
of services, most of these deal with procedural questions and with
standards to be met, rather than the essential question, "Why purchase?"
In the opinion of the authors, there are no consistent policies governing
purchase of services except those that have evolved out of the pre-
Title XX program and those stemming from prevalent political and community
pressures. Table 35 illustrates the range of replies received from key
state individuals in the eight states and the perceptions of the federal
regional office staff responsible for each of the 50 states and the
District of Columbia. The senior state administrators of provider
agencies surveyed were asked similar questions. Their replies are shown
in tables 36 and 37.

F.  CONCLUSION

In spite of a number of aspects of Title XX which would tend to
inhibit change in the allocation of social services resources, changes
appear to have occurred. Among the more prominent effects of Title XX
have been the following:

1.  An expansion in the services program of states which were not at
their ceiling prior to Title XX, while the programs of states at ceiling
have been relatively unaffected.

TABLE 35

Criteria Used to Decide Whether a Particular Service
Should Be Provided Directly or Purchased

|  | Key State Respondents % of Total | Regional Office Staff % of Total |
|---|---|---|
| Community Pressure/Politics | 17 | 16 |
| Ability to Provide Service Directly | 12 | 18 |
| Tradition | 18 | 10 |
| Availability of Staff | 13 | 13 |
| Cost | 11 | 11 |
| Match Availability | 8 | 12 |
| Availability of Provider/Source | 12 | 7 |
| Staff Expertise | 3 | 6 |
| Other | 6 | 7 |
| Total | 100% | 100% |

Source: The Urban Institute Title XX Study: 8 State In-Depth Survey and HEW Regional Office Survey

Note: State and regional office respondents were provided an opportunity to indicate more than one criterion.

115

TABLE 36

Criteria Which Apply to State Agency Decisions in Contracting
for a Service Rather Than Providing the Service Directly
(Senior State Administrator Perceptions)

|  | Percent of Responses | | | |
|---|---|---|---|---|
|  | Required Criteria | Preferred Criteria | Does Not Apply | Total |
| When qualified SSD staff are not available | 19 | 61 | 20 | 100 |
| When other public and private agencies have traditionally provided the services themselves | 17 | 56 | 27 | 100 |
| When a service is discrete, tangible, or where unit costs can readily be determined | 16 | 46 | 38 | 100 |
| When there is an absolute shortage of SSD staff without regard to qualifications | 11 | 37 | 52 | 100 |
| When the cost of contracted service is less than for direct services | 9 | 52 | 39 | 100 |
| In order to finance a service which was previously provided, but not under Title XX | 9 | 36 | 55 | 100 |
| When other criteria influence a decision in favor of contracted services | 30 | 37 | 33 | 100 |

Source:  The Urban Institue Title XX Study:  Purchased Services Provider Administrator Survey

Note:  Senior State Administrators were asked to assess the use of each criterion.

TABLE 37

Factors Which Influenced Single State Agency to Contract
with Provider Rather Than Provide Service Directly
(Administrator of Provider Agency Perceptions)

| | Applies | | Does Not Apply | | Total | |
|---|---|---|---|---|---|---|
| | # | % | # | % | # | % |
| Because the agency had traditionally provided the service | 108 | 83 | 22 | 17 | 130 | 100 |
| Because qualified SSD staff were not available | 74 | 63 | 44 | 37 | 118 | 100 |
| Because the cost of contracted service was less than for direct services | 71 | 58 | 51 | 42 | 122 | 100 |
| In order to finance a service which was previously provided but not under Title XX | 65 | 55 | 53 | 45 | 118 | 100 |
| Because the service was discrete, tangible, or unit costs could readily be determined | 61 | 53 | 55 | 47 | 116 | 100 |
| Because there was an absolute shortage of SSD staff without regard to qualifications | 38 | 34 | 73 | 66 | 111 | 100 |
| Because of other criteria | 27 | 45 | 33 | 55 | 60 | 100 |

Source: The Urban Institute Title XX Study: Purchased Services Provider
Administrator Survey

Note: Provider administrators were asked to assess the use of each criterion.

2. Perhaps as a result of resource restrictions, less than a third of all states have opted for the maximum income eligibility levels permitted by federal legislation, and a substantial minority of states have further opted to reduce client eligibility levels since the inception of Title XX.

3. Although there has been a continuation of services to persons who received services under Titles IV-A and VI, there has also been an increase in the number of income eligible individuals receiving social services.

4. Very limited data suggest that minorities and women receive a larger share of social services than their proportion of the population eligible for Title XX services would suggest.

5. Similarly limited data indicate that the aging receive a fair share of Title XX services nationally.

6. Examination of state-level data only tend to obscure often dramatic shifts in the substate allocation and reallocation of social services resources.

7. Perhaps the most dramatic shift brought about by Title XX implementation is the dramatic increase in purchased services (compared to those provided directly by the SSD). Purchased services are now the predominant mode of service delivery nationally.

## V.  ORGANIZING AND MANAGING SOCIAL SERVICES

A.  INTRODUCTION

This chapter examines the effects of Title XX of the Social Security Act on the organization and management of state social service departments (SSDs).  This analysis assumes special importance when it is realized that, by and large, effects on state agency organization and management were not explicitly intended by the framers of Title XX.  Nevertheless, it appears that implementation of this legislation has substantially, if unintentionally, affected the state-level administration of social service programs.  This chapter examines the special impact of Title XX's implementation on organizational structure, processes, and staffing.

In addition to examining the overall effects of Title XX on state agency organization and management, this paper addresses the following, more specific questions:

o What changes in the backgrounds, skills, and qualifications required of state agency personnel have been effected by Title XX?

o How responsive have state training and staff development programs been to changing manpower requirements?

o What effects have Title XX had on state reporting systems, on paperwork, and on state personnel?

o What effect has Title XX had on purchase of service and what impact has purchase of service had on state organization and management?

The effects of Title XX on state agency organization and management in the eight states studied in-depth are summarized in table 38.  These data, together with those in table 39, indicate that Title XX is seen by regional- and state-level respondents as having had a significant effect on the organization and management of state social services agencies.  The most significant changes have occurred in organizational structure, personnel, training, and information systems.

TABLE 38

Effects of Title XX on Organization and Management in Eight States

| State | Title XX Unit | Purchase-of-Service Unit | Info. Systems | Decentralization | Other Major Reorganization | No. of SSD Directors since 1975 |
|---|---|---|---|---|---|---|
| | | | Creation of or Major Changes in: | | | |
| Arizona | Yes | Yes | No | Yes | Yes | 2 |
| California | Yes | No | No | No | Yes | 2 |
| Iowa | Yes | Yes | Yes | Yes | No | 2 |
| Michigan | Yes | Yes | Yes | Yes | Yes | 1 |
| New York | Yes | No | Yes | No | Yes | 5 |
| North Carolina | Yes | Yes | Yes | Yes | Yes | 3 |
| Oregon | Yes | No | Yes | No | Yes | 2 |
| Texas | Yes | Yes | Yes | Yes | Yes | 2 |

Source: The Urban Institute Title XX Study: 8 State In-Depth Study.

TABLE 39

Overall Impact of Title XX on State Agency
Organization and Management

| Scale/ Value | Extent of Impact | Regional Office Instrument | | In-Depth Interviews | |
|---|---|---|---|---|---|
| | | Relative Frequency | | Relative Frequency | |
| | | No. of States | Percent of Total | No. of Responses | Percent of Total |
| 1 | Little or none | 3 | 6.0 | 24 | 18.7 |
| 2 | Less than moderate | 7 | 14.0 | 13 | 10.2 |
| 3 | Moderate | 21 | 42.0 | 35 | 27.3 |
| 4 | More than moderate | 12 | 24.0 | 32 | 25.0 |
| 5 | Major | 7 | 14.0 | 24 | 18.8 |
| -- | No response | 1 | -- | -- | -- |
| | Total | 51 | 100.0 | 128 | 100.0 |
| | Average assessment | | 3.3 | | 3.0 |

Sources:  The Urban Institute Title XX Study:  8 State In-Depth Study;
The Urban Institute Title XX Study:  HEW Regional Office Survey.

B.   CHANGES IN ORGANIZATIONAL STRUCTURE

Table 40 presents data regarding changes in the organizational structure of state social services agencies from the perspective of senior state administrators and HEW regional office staff.  The changes most frequently attributed to Title XX are discussed below.

1.   Establishment or Upgrading of Planning and Evaluation Units within the State Agency

Thirty states were reported to have created or upgraded their planning and evaluation units since the implementation of Title XX.  The responses of senior state administrators in 19 states suggest that this has primarily involved the creation of planning units.  Based on the experience of eight states studied by The Urban Institute, which have all created or upgraded their planning units since Title XX's implementation, such units most often bear the prime responsibility for the Comprehensive Annual Services Program (CASP) planning process mandated by Title XX.  In 14 states, Title XX planning units are, or are likely to be, responsible for planning, needs assessments, monitoring, and management.

2.   Establishment of a Purchase of Service Unit

In 16 states a separate unit has been created to administer services provided under contract to the SSD.  Regional offices expect that another seven states will create separate purchase of service units within the next three years.  Purchase units were created in six of the eight states studied by The Urban Institute.  It may be significant that the only two states which do not have such offices are states in which purchased services are administered by county social services agencies.

TABLE 40

Changes in SSD Structure Attributable to Title XX

| | Senior State Admin. a (No. of Responses) | | | | Regional Office Survey b (No. of Jurisdictions) | | | |
|---|---|---|---|---|---|---|---|---|
| | To Date | | Within Three Years | | To Date | | Within Three Years | |
| | Yes | No | Yes | No | Yes | No | Yes | No |
| Establishing or upgrading of planning and evaluation units within the state agency | -- | -- | -- | -- | 30 | 10 | 23 | 4 |
| Establishment of a planning unit for Title XX funded social services | 150 | 30 | 28 | 16 | -- | -- | -- | -- |
| Upgrading of a planning unit for Title XX funded social services | 74 | 54 | 81 | 21 | -- | -- | -- | -- |
| Establishment of an evaluation unit for Title XX funded social services | 74 | 72 | 90 | 21 | -- | -- | -- | -- |
| Upgrading of an evaluation unit for Title XX funded social services | 32 | 78 | 78 | 39 | -- | -- | -- | -- |
| Establishment of a self-contained Title XX unit within the SSD, responsible for all Title XX related functions (e.g., planning, needs assessment, monitoring, and management) | 82 | 78 | 33 | 69 | 8 | 31 | 6 | 18 |
| Establishment of a purchase-of-service unit within the SSD or its regional offices | 130 | 52 | 16 | 32 | 16 | 23 | 7 | 14 |
| Decentralization of responsibility for policy formulation for social services | 46 | 117 | 33 | 81 | 9 | 30 | 7 | 15 |
| Changed relationships between the SSD and other human service agencies (e.g., state agency on aging | 111 | 52 | 62 | 24 | 27 | 12 | 20 | 5 |
| Establishment of a separate services eligibility determination unit | 56 | 106 | 32 | 61 | -- | -- | -- | -- |
| Establishment of a separate services reporting or monitoring unit | 97 | 66 | 51 | 34 | -- | -- | -- | -- |
| Other organizational changes including expansion of internal audit, legal, and management information functions | 98 | 56 | 91 | 14 | 27 | 12 | 20 | 5 |

Sources:  The Urban Institute Title XX Study:  Senior Social Services Administrator Survey; The Urban Institute Title XX Study: HEW Regional Office Survey

a.  n = 196

b.  n = 51 (50 states and the District of Columbia).  Regional offices reported that no changes in SSD structure attributable to Title XX had occurred in 11 states or were likely to occur within the next three years in 17 jurisdictions.

3.  Changed Relationships Between the SSD and Other Human Resource Agencies

In over half of all states (from the perspective of HEW regional offices) and in the opinion of over two-thirds of the senior state administrators surveyed, relationships between the SSD and other human resources agencies have changed as a result of Title XX's implementation.

Based on the findings of The Urban Institute eight-state study, the most significant changes involved increased integration of human resources programs through cooperative agreements (e.g., with state agencies on aging), purchase of service contracts with other states agencies, joint funding, and intertitle transfers. Other SSD organizational changes reported or observed included the expansion of internal audit, legal, or management information functions.

Although less apparent from the regional office and senior state administrator perspectives, significant trends toward decentralization were drafted in five of the states studied by the Institute. These shifts, though not wholly the result of Title XX, are at least facilitated by the opportunity (not present prior to 1975) to engage in substate planning for social services.

C.  CHANGES IN PERSONNEL

One of the most fundamental ways in which the federal government can affect SSD organization and management is by changing the nature of professional backgrounds, skills, or qualifications of the people responsible for administering or delivering social services. Little in Title XX itself, its regulations, or other material pertaining to the law mandates or even suggests that a change in the nature of staffing is appropriate. Nevertheless, changes in those skills may be deemed necessary to the extent that Title XX is perceived to present new challenges or requirements which cannot be met by the existing workforce.

Conversely, the demand for persons with other skills may be diminished or eliminated altogether by changes in service priorities or program emphasis.

As suggested by table 41, Title XX is perceived to have increased the demand for persons with backgrounds in planning (44 states), evaluation (39 states), data processing (33 states), statistics and reporting (33 states), and contract administration (32 states). These shifts are consistent with the new requirements of the CASP planning process and a continued desire to upgrade state evaluation capacity of social service agencies. These data also reflect the growth of purchased (vs. direct) services.

The skills, backgrounds, and qualifications which were relatively unaffected by Title XX or for which demand was perceived as declining were direct service delivery and services eligibility. Declining demand for the latter skill is somewhat surprising, since Title XX initially required several states to establish individual eligibility processes for social services.

D. TRAINING AND STAFF DEVELOPMENT

Most states have had to manage Title XX with the basic staff they had prior to its implementation. Unless additional resources become available, the principal responses to changed staffing needs are likely to be reorganization, personnel detail or shifting assignments, and staff training and retraining. The data presented as table 42 indicate, however, that state training programs have been only moderately responsive to changing manpower needs. Respondents in the eight states studied by The Urban Institute were even more critical of the relevance (or irrelevance) of state training programs.

TABLE 41

Effects of Title XX on Personnel,
Qualifications, or Skills Needed to
Deliver or Administer Social Services

|  | Number of States | | |
| Skill | Less Demand | No Change | More Demand |
| --- | --- | --- | --- |
| Planning | -- | 1 | 44 |
| Evaluation | -- | 3 | 39 |
| Administration | -- | 17 | 23 |
| Case Management | 1 | 17 | 33 |
| Contract Administration | -- | 9 | 32 |
| Data Processing | -- | 9 | 33 |
| Accounting, Audit | -- | 14 | 25 |
| Statistics and Reporting | -- | 9 | 33 |
| Services Eligibility | 4 | 17 | 19 |
| Direct Service Delivery | 4 | 26 | 9 |

Source:  The Urban Institute Title XX Study: HEW Regional Office Survey.

TABLE 42

Responsiveness of SSD Training Programs:
Need for Changes in Personnel, Skills, or Qualifications

| | | | Number of States | |
| Degree of Responsiveness | Scale/ Value | Absolute Frequency | Absolute Frequency (Percent) | Adjusted Frequency (Percent) |
| --- | --- | --- | --- | --- |
| Not at all | 1.00 | 5 | 9.8 | 10.4 |
| Less than moderately | 2.00 | 10 | 19.6 | 20.8 |
| Moderately | 3.00 | 22 | 43.1 | 45.8 |
| More than moderately | 4.00 | 8 | 15.7 | 16.7 |
| Fully | 5.00 | 3 | 5.9 | 6.3 |
| No response | 0.0 | 3 | 5.9 | -- |
| Total | | 51 | 100.0 | 100.0 |

Mean response: 2.9

Source: The Urban Institute Title XX Study: HEW Regional Office Survey.

The data presented in table 43 reflect the nature of state training programs and the areas in which senior state administrators, administrators of provider agencies, and social service workers believe training is most appropriate.

The major areas in which training for SSD staff has been offered include services eligibility, service technology, statistics and reporting, planning and administration. The only two training areas in which more than half of all service workers polled participated were services eligibility and services to families, children, and adults.

These data also suggest that the major areas in which training may not have kept pace with skill demands include program evaluation, case management, administration (in the opinion of managers), and contract management (in the opinion of service workers).

E.   STATISTICS AND REPORTING

As indicated by the data presented in table 44, the statistics, reporting, and data processing functions are the administrative processes most heavily affected by the implementation of Title XX. Based on the Institute's eight-state examination, these data may reflect the impact on state information systems of Title XX's Social Services Reporting Requirements (SSRR). At the end of the first year of Title XX's implementation, 20 states had created or significantly modified their reporting systems.

A primary concern during Title XX's first year of operation was the paperwork the legislation involved. Newspaper headlines concerning Title XX included references to "Obstacle Course for Welfare," "Helping Hands Tied Up By Red Tape," and "$60,000 Grant Not Worth The Paperwork."

TABLE 43

Provision of Training and Perceived Training Needs

| | | Has SSD provided training in each area in the last year?[a] | | | Within the past year have you participated in training dealing with the following areas?[b] | | | In which of the following areas do you think training would be the most appropriate? Number of Responses (Rank) | | |
| | | No. of Responses | | | No. of Responses | | | Senior State Administ.[a] | Social Service Workers[b] | Provider Administ.[c] |
| | | Yes | No | % Yes | Yes | No | % Yes | | | |
|---|---|---|---|---|---|---|---|---|---|---|
| (1) | Planning | 90 | 55 | 62.1 | 38 | 158 | 19.4 | 112 (3) | 57 (5) | 63 (3) |
| (2) | Evaluation | 60 | 71 | 45.8 | 43 | 152 | 22.0 | 147 (1) | 60 (4) | 74 (1) |
| (3) | Administration | 84 | 58 | 59.2 | 21 | 170 | 11.0 | 99 (6) | 23 (8) | 55 (4) |
| (4) | Case Management | 74 | 61 | 54.8 | 80 | 123 | 39.4 | 119 (2) | 104 (2) | 55 (4) |
| (5) | Contract Administration | 72 | 70 | 50.7 | 20 | 170 | 10.5 | 93 (7) | 24 (7) | 44 (8) |
| (6) | Data Processing | 45 | 85 | 34.6 | 33 | 159 | 17.1 | 66 (10) | 12 (10) | 21 (10) |
| (7) | Accounting, Audit | 52 | 74 | 41.3 | 16 | 172 | 8.5 | 72 (9) | 13 (9) | 43 (9) |
| (8) | Statistics and Reporting | 89 | 48 | 65.0 | 69 | 129 | 34.8 | 100 (5) | 32 (6) | 49 (6) |
| (9) | Services Eligibility | 119 | 29 | 80.4 | 123 | 85 | 59.1 | 83 (8) | 65 (3) | 46 (7) |
| (10) | Social Services to Families, Children and/or Adults | 119 | 31 | 79.3 | 173 | 46 | 79.0 | 109 (4) | 182 (1) | 73 (2) |
| (11) | Other Title XX Related Training | 47 | 36 | 56.6 | 33 | 55 | 37.5 | 24 (11) | 12 (10) | 10 (11) |

a. The Urban Institute Title XX Study: Senior Social Services Administrator Survey.
b. The Urban Institute Title XX Study: Social Service Workers Survey.
c. The Urban Institute Title XX Study: Survey of Administrators of Provider Agencies.

TABLE 44

Effects of Title XX Implementation on Selected
Administrative Functions or Processes

| Function or Process | Number of Jurisdictions[a] | | | | | Mean Response |
| --- | --- | --- | --- | --- | --- | --- |
| | Little or No Change 1 | Less than Moderate Change 2 | Moderate Change 3 | More than Moderate Change 4 | Major Change 5 | |
| Financial Accounting | 8 | 10 | 14 | 11 | 3 | 2.8 |
| Statistics or Reporting | 3 | 5 | 13 | 18 | 12 | 3.6 |
| Data Processing | 6 | 7 | 17 | 11 | 10 | 3.2 |
| Training | 6 | 15 | 16 | 10 | 4 | 2.8 |
| Legislative | 15 | 13 | 12 | 10 | 1 | 2.4 |

Source: The Urban Institute Title XX Study: HEW Regional Office Survey.
a. Forty-six of the fifty-one regional offices responded to this question.

Concerns about paperwork seem to have abated substantially during the second year of Title XX's implementation. This may have partially resulted from the reduction of federal reporting requirements (e.g., elimination of requirements for individual basic data files), state accommodation of worker concerns, or simply the fact that workers became more accustomed to the new reporting demands of Title XX. Overall, the legacy of SSRR has been an enhanced information systems capacity. In five of the eight states examined by the Institute, new social services information systems were developed or existing systems substantially modified, largely in response to Title XX requirements.

F.    NET EFFECTS ON THE ALLOCATION OF WORKER TIME

One of the most significant measures of the internal effects of Title XX on state agency organization and management is the legislation's net effects on the allocation of time spent on various tasks by those who deal daily on a face-to-face basis with the consumers of social services--social service line workers. Table 45 presents the adjusted percentages of time social service workers reported spending on various functions prior to 1975 and at the time the survey was completed, in the spring of 1977. While in no sense can these data be interpreted as a time study, they do suggest that some changes may have taken place, at least from the perspective of service workers who held positions in 1977 comparable to those they held prior to 1975.

The most significant shifts suggested by these data are substantial increases in the amount of caseworker time spent on eligibility determination and redetermination, reporting, and case management. These increases are offset largely by reductions in direct service delivery and lessened responsibilities for income maintenance functions.

TABLE 45

Allocation of Service Workers' Time in 1977
vs. Pre-1975 Allocation

| Function | Adjusted Percentage of Time[a] | | |
| | Prior to 1975 | 1977 | Difference |
|---|---|---|---|
| Eligibility determination or redetermination for social services | 8.7 | 12.4 | + 3.7 |
| Eligibility determination or redetermination for income maintenance (i.e., public assistance, food stamps, and/or medical assistance | 14.6 | 7.5 | - 7.1 |
| Statistics and reports to management (excluding maintenance of case records) | 6.4 | 9.8 | + 3.4 |
| Case management (including maintenance of case records) | 16.0 | 21.2 | + 5.2 |
| Direct delivery of social services to clients (i.e., foster care, homemaker, counseling, day care, or protective services) | 45.0 | 39.0 | - 6.0 |
| In-service training | 3.9 | 4.5 | + 0.6 |
| Other (e.g., staff meetings and general conferences) | 5.4 | 5.6 | + 0.2 |
| Total | 100.0 | 100.0 | -- |

Source: The Urban Institute Title XX Study: Social Services Workers' Survey.
a. Times adjusted to total 100.0 percent. Raw values for the pre-1975 and 1977 periods totalled 122 and 116 percent respectively.

G.  CONCLUSION

As may be the case with most data, those presented concerning the effects of Title XX on SSD organization and management can be interpreted in a variety of ways.  In the opinion of the authors, however, the following policy implications appear most significant:

1.  State social services agencies are an extremely unstable setting for program administration.

Although comparable data for the period prior to 1975 are not available, it appears that the rapidity with which changes in organizational form and leadership are taking place within SSDs is increasing.

As indicated in table 38, all but one of the eight states examined by The Urban Institute have changed directors since the inception of Title XX, and only one other has avoided a substantial reorganization during the past two and a half years.  In other words, each of the eight states has either undertaken a massive reorganization, adjusted to new leadership, or (more likely) both, in addition to implementing Title XX.

Although it is not suggested that all change is undesirable, there are a number of negative consequences of administrative instability.  These include:

o  A number of false starts in management information systems. According to findings from the eight-state study, the support of top management is particularly crucial to the development of social services and management information systems.  The pet project of one SSD director may become a "white elephant" under his or her successor.  Inordinate turnover may result, then, in a number of false starts in information systems development, increasing the cynicism of local offices, provider agencies, and line workers about the value of paperwork the SSD requires them to perform.

o <u>Discontinuity in agency policy</u>. In one state, for example, one director was moving the agency toward case management, his successor was indifferent to this policy, and a third has charted a new course.

o <u>An environment not particularly conducive to evaluation</u>. Most major evaluation studies are multi-year endeavors. Even where shorter-term studies are more appropriate, they may be best conducted within an overall framework which has some consistency and durability. Rapid turnover and constant organizational flux seldom permit the development and use of such evaluative frameworks.

o <u>Frequent reorganizations intended to increase accountability may actually diminish public and agency accountability</u>. A continuing concern in the administration of social services is accountability (i.e., concerns with regard to political action, ideology, policy-making, program effectiveness, and professional responsibility). As suggested above, the prime instrument of accountability afforded by Title XX, the CASP planning process, is seriously deficient as a means of accountability. In the absence of continuity in agency leadership, the lack of a viable formal means of public accountability is even more important than it might otherwise be.

2. <u>Changes in the structure of SSD organization may mask more fundamental problems</u>.

In many respects, changes in organizational structure are a "quick fix." If an agency is presented with a new responsibility--for example, the CASP planning process--the simplest way to deal with the challenge is to create a CASP planning unit. If a state agency has a problem with contracted services, it may be very tempted to create a purchase of service unit (even though the

implications of having most of the SSD programs administered by such an agency
may not have been considered).  If these initial steps do not solve the problem,
the agency may look toward still further reorganization as the solution.

Although restructuring an agency may be one means of meeting the changing
challenges faced by social services agencies, complete and total reliance
on structural changes may prevent those agencies from recognizing (and, in
fact, may obscure) fundamental and complex administrative problems.

The data presented in this and other papers, in the opinion of the authors,
suggest that the administration of social services today is substantially
different than it was ten years ago.  Social services are now a multi-billion
dollar industry involving public and private agencies other than traditional
public welfare departments.  The backgrounds, qualifications, and skills
required of individuals responsible for managing and delivering social services
have also changed; reorganization, however, does not necessarily assure that
these new requirements will be met.

3.  <u>Federal and, for the most part, state leadership do not see the
lack of management training as a significant problem</u>.

The lack of management training is not a problem of inadequate <u>supply</u>.
There are public and private institutions capable of providing training in the
skill areas required as a result of Title XX implementation.  Rather, the
reason these resources are not applied appears to be a lack of <u>demand</u> for such
training on the part of SSD leadership.

National data on state management training programs do not exist.  Thus,
the federal government has no comprehensive overview of the types of training
being provided by individual states.  State training plans which were previously
required under Title XX regulations, although admittedly inadequate, were

abolished instead of improved. As a result, the federal role in sharing common course programs, stimulating new training initiatives, and assessing the value of existing services has been seriously impaired.

4. <u>State data capabilities, enhanced by Title XX, are greater than generally recognized</u>.

Although serious problems of credibility and integrity exist with SSRR, states often have an internal capability greater than that indicated by the nature of the data they share with the federal government. It is somewhat ironic that the data states provide under SSRR are often regarded as being "for federal purposes only," and that the states insist that the data they utilize for their own decision-making purposes meet a higher standard of reliability than those they provide to the federal government.

It appears from the authors' work with quantitative cost, client, and service data in five states that considerable additional insight may be obtained from investigating the state data systems which support the SSRR data. Although there are considerable difficulties in making cross-state (or even inter-year) comparisons, it does appear that states are capable of and are making greater investments in information systems than those required of them by the federal government.

It does not appear, however, that these data are being used as management tools, except perhaps for fiscal analyses. Data have to be analyzed, not just collected, and SSD management must be trained in their use for analysis and decision-making.

5. <u>The organization and management implications of dramatic growth in purchased services have generally failed to be recognized</u>.

The administrative regulations, management structure, and service staff of most SSDs reflect this failure. In systems that rely primarily on purchased services, the skills of contract administration, evaluation, monitoring and case management become as important as service delivery skills.  However, although the nature of public social services has changed drastically, the training of staff in contract management, case management, and related fields has apparently not been keeping pace.

Contracting and contract administration place new demands on the administrators of provider agencies, both public and private, as well as on state agency staff.  Paradoxically, current Title XX training regulations prohibit the use of Title XX funds for the training of non-SSD administrators.

## VI. CHANGING ROLES AND RESPONSIBILITIES IN THE PROVISION OF SOCIAL SERVICES

### A. INTRODUCTION

A major goal in the formulation of Title XX of the Social Security Act was to eliminate the open conflict which characterized federal-state relations from 1972 to 1976. According to an earlier Urban Institute study, legislation like Title XX offered

> the possibility of shifting the focus of intergovernmental negotiation from how things are done to the current condition of those who are the object of the social services. . . . The genius of special revenue sharing becomes its capacity to focus the federal government on nationally valued ends while state and local governments are given maximum flexibility in adopting means calculated to achieve them.

This chapter examines the effects of Title XX on relations between the states and the national government in the administration of the nation's social services. Specifically, the following questions will be addressed:

o What has been the effect of Title XX implementation on federal-state working relationships?

o What has been the nature and extent of federal regional office support and assistance to state social services departments (SSDs)?

o What is the perceived effect of federal fiscal accountability requirements on state social services programs?

o To what extent do states take preventive measures to limit the potential for audit exceptions or federal fiscal sanctions?

In spite of the eagerness of the federal government and the states to alter the nature of their relationship, a number of factors existed at the start of Title XX's implementation which have restricted its potential ameliorative effect on federal-state relations.

1. No "New" Money

The $2.5 billion annual ceiling on federal social services authorizations which was imposed in 1972 remains in effect. As more and more states approach their ceiling, Title XX has increasingly been viewed as a source of funding for existing programs. Further, in the face of inflation and, in some instances, declines in population relative to other states, the federal allowance to states is actually smaller than it had been previously. To the extent that Title XX funds are seen as the same "old" money, it is unlikely that states' attitudes toward the use of those funds will change.

2. Short Lead Time

By all accounts, the implementation of Title XX during the first year was accomplished on essentially a "crash" basis. Because of the short time available to all parties, states and regional offices had little opportunity to jointly think through the changes in their respective roles brought about by Title XX. Priority in most instances appeared to be given to questions of task (e.g., getting the CASP plan out) rather than maintenance functions (e.g., the reformulation of roles). In addition, the short time available for implementation acted as a barrier to role shifts at the regional offices because it encouraged HEW's central office and the states to deal directly with one another, in effect bypassing the regional office staff.

### 3. Same State and Federal Staff

Partially as a result of the factors cited above, states and regional offices had basically the same staff available to them during Title XX's first year of implementation as they had had previously. This meant that state and federal counterparts tended to interact as they had previously and that staff skills and competencies (e.g., fiscal or programmatic orientations) are likely to restrict dramatic departures from the status quo.

### 4. Bureaucratic Machinery

Both public parties (namely, the states and the federal government) to the implementation of Title XX were the same as they had been under previous titles. Each had the same tools available to them (e.g., regulations, audits, manuals, and other issuances) as they had previously. Further, Title XX was not the only basis of interaction between most SSDs and the HEW regional offices. SSDs typically administer public assistance and Medicaid, which were not a part of "New Federalism." Thus, the likelihood of a changing federal-state relationship with regard to a single program (like Title XX) was inhibited by interactions with regard to other programs.

## B. EFFECT OF TITLE XX ON FEDERAL-STATE WORKING RELATIONSHIPS

To assess the extent to which working relations between state agencies and the national government had moved from the hostility which often characterized the pre-Title XX period, senior state officials in eight states and respondents in each of HEW's ten regional offices were asked the same question:

> Has Title XX resulted in improved or worsened working relationships between the state and the federal regional office?

Responses were made on a five-point scale with values ranging from 1 (indicating much worse) to 5 (indicating much better). These data are presented in table 46.

From the perspective of federal regional offices, working relations are better or much better in over two-thirds of the states. No regional office respondents indicated that federal-state working relations were worse.

State-level responses were less positive. Still, nearly half of all state responses indicated that relations were improved, and less than 17 percent expressed the view that federal-state working relations had deteriorated as a result of Title XX's implementation.

These data are consistent with an apparent change in federal regional office orientation under Title XX (i.e., placing less emphasis on compliance and monitoring of state activities, instead adopting more supportive roles as providers of technical assistance). Relations may be further enhanced by the recent settlement of litigation around retroactive purchase of service claims. Outstanding state claims for disallowed federal reimbursement, dating back to 1972, were observed as having clouded relationships between many states and the federal government.

## C.   FEDERAL REGIONAL OFFICE SUPPORT AND ASSISTANCE

Federal assistance to states during the first year of Title XX's implementation consisted mainly of aid in producing the state CASP plans required by Title XX. Based on Urban Institute observations, regional office technical assistance in 28 states during that period centered on plan preparation, plan

TABLE 46

Effect of Title XX on Federal-State
Working Relationships

| Scale/ Value | Response | 8-State Responses | | Regional Office Instrument | |
|---|---|---|---|---|---|
| | | No. of Responses | Percent Of Total | No. of States | Percent Of Total |
| 1 | Much Worse | 2 | 3.4 | -- | 0.0 |
| 2 | Worse | 8 | 12.5 | -- | 0.0 |
| 3 | No Change | 21 | 35.6 | 16 | 31.4 |
| 4 | Better | 21 | 35.6 | 23 | 45.1 |
| 5 | Much Better | 7 | 11.9 | 12 | 23.5 |
| | | 59 | 100.0 | 51 | 100.0 |
| | AVERAGE ASSESSMENT | | 3.4 | | 3.9 |

Sources: The Urban Institute Title XX Study: 8 State In-Depth Study and The Urban Institute Title XX Study:
HEW Regional Office Survey

amendment, needs assessment, services reporting (SSRR implementation), and service eligibility procedures. In 14 states, regional office assistance consisted of policy interpretation and resolution of issues regarding federal fiscal participation (FFP). A separate, internal study by HEW indicated that

> the major focus of the first year's technical assistance effort was in the areas of program planning and evaluation. States were required to develop and publish their CASP before the beginning of the first program year. . . . 20 of the 22 HEW units which provided technical assistance did so in the area of program planning, with 17 units assisting states with evaluation concerns.

During the second year of Title XX's implementation, regional office support and assistance appears to have focused substantially less on CASP plan production. Three observations are relevant in this regard:

1. Type and Utility of Support and Assistance

The primary focus of regional office support to state social services agencies during the second year of Title XX appears to have been policy interpretation, financial management, interagency coordination, program reporting, purchase of service management, and general technical assistance. Responses were made on a five-point scale with values ranging from 1 (indicating little or none) to 5 (indicating a great deal). These data are presented in table 47. The data collected from the in-depth study states suggest that the volume of such assistance has increased since the first year. Both groups of respondents report that regional office assistance has increased sharply since the implementation of Title XX.

It is interesting that state and federal priorities for technical assistance (i.e., that assistance deemed "most useful") are generally

TABLE 47

Nature and Extent of Federal Regional Office Support and Assistance

| Area of Support/Assistance | 8 State Survey | | | | Regional Office Instrument | | | |
|---|---|---|---|---|---|---|---|---|
| | Pre-Title XX | First Year | Second Year | Most Useful | Pre-Title XX | First Year | Second Year | Most Useful |
| Program Evaluation | 1.6 | 2.3 | 3.0 | 2 | 1.9 | 2.5 | 3.1 | 1 |
| Policy Interpretation | 2.5 | 3.7 | 4.3 | 1 | 3.6 | 4.3 | 4.2 | 2 |
| Organization Design | 1.0 | 1.5 | 2.7 | 9 | 1.6 | 1.9 | 1.9 | 10 |
| Needs Assessment | 1.0 | 1.7 | 3.0 | 6 | 1.4 | 2.3 | 2.4 | 7 |
| Purchase of Service | 1.0 | 1.5 | 3.0 | 6 | 2.8 | 3.3 | 3.4 | 4 |
| Program Reporting | 1.0 | 3.0 | 4.0 | 4 | 2.2 | 3.0 | 3.1 | 5 |
| Service Inventory | 1.0 | 1.0 | 3.0 | 9 | 1.8 | 2.3 | 2.3 | 9 |
| Financial Management | 1.0 | 2.0 | 3.5 | 6 | 2.8 | 3.1 | 3.1 | 6 |
| Interagency Coordination | 1.0 | 2.5 | 3.3 | 4 | 2.0 | 2.8 | 2.9 | 8 |
| General Technical Assistance | 1.0 | 2.5 | 3.3 | 3 | 3.3 | 3.9 | 4.0 | 3 |
| Average Assessment | 1.3 | 2.3 | 3.4 | -- | 2.3 | 2.9 | 3.0 | -- |

Sources: The Urban Institute Title XX Study: 8 State In-Depth Study; The Urban Institute
Title XX Study: HEW Regional Office Survey.

consistent. This may be attributable to the fact that over two-thirds of all federal technical assistance is provided at the request of state agencies. The areas of support or assistance seen as being most useful by state and regional office respondents are program evaluation, policy interpretation, and general technical assistance. The single area of support where state and federal perceptions of utility are sharply divergent is interagency coordination, an area of support viewed as considerably more useful by state respondents than by regional office respondents.

2. Sufficiency of Support

Though the volume of assistance given by the federal government has increased considerably in the second year and its usefulness is widely acknowledged by both state and regional offices, nearly half of all HEW offices providing technical assistance are dissatisfied with the level of support they are able to provide. As indicated from the data presented in table 48, 10 of 23 offices providing technical support and assistance to states during the first year of Title XX felt that their staffs were too small and/or lacked sufficient expertise to meet their responsibilities.

TABLE 48

Sufficiency of Federal Technical Assistance
Staff in Relation to Needs

| Sufficiency of Staff | Total # | Total % |
|---|---|---|
| Number of offices reporting staff sufficient | 13 | 57 |
| Number of offices reporting staff not sufficient | 10 | 43 |
| | 23 | 100 |

Those offices that felt they lacked an adequate staff (in terms of size, expertise, or both), indicated that they most critically needed program specialists, evaluation and monitoring staff, service and training staff, and contractors/consultants.

3. Targeting of Assistance

In addition to the fact that some regional office personnel felt that they are unable to give as much assistance as they would like to the states, there is evidence that what assistance is given may not be appropriately targeted. The bulk of federal technical assistance is provided to staffs of state social service agencies, although more than half of all Title XX-funded social services are provided by private and public agencies other than the SSDs. Some federal assistance is also provided to governors' offices and state legislators.

D. FISCAL ACCOUNTABILITY REQUIREMENTS

A number of federal regulations exist to assure that Title XX funds are legally and appropriately spent. An enduring issue in intergovernmental relations is the effect of the regulatory "strings" attached to grant-in-aid funds.

One of the most highly touted features of "special revenue sharing" programs, in contrast to more categorical forms of grant-in-aid programs, is the relative absence of strings. During 1973, states engaged the federal government in the "battle of the regs," protesting HEW's social services regulations, which were termed a case of "bureaucratic strangulation." It may have been natural, then, for some observers to believe that the Title XX legislation, having emerged from this period of turmoil, would be self-implementing

or "regulation-free."

In this context, the outcry over the initial set of proposed Title XX

regulations was understandable. The final regulations governing the initial

year of Title XX's implementation were considerably less rigorous in terms

of expectations for client eligibility, contracting, and scope of eligible

social services than those initially proposed. In the end, it was HEW's

view that even a program like Title XX required fiscal accountability regu-

lations (i.e., stipulations to assure that funds are legally and appropriately

spent).

In order to compare the perspectives of federal regional offices with

those of senior state officials, each group was asked to assess the effect

of federal fiscal accountability requirements on three aspects of state

social service programs--state administrative capacity, service delivery,

and state agency monitoring and evaluation. The data presented as table 49

indicate that the perspectives of the two groups were in fairly sharp con-

trast; regional offices consistently felt that federal fiscal accountability

requirements had a more positive effect on state social services programs

than did the state-level respondents.

In spite of this difference of opinion, state and regional perspectives

were consistent with regard to the relative effect of federal fiscal accounta-

bility requirements. That is, respondents felt that Title XX regulations

had the most positive (or least negative) effects on SSD monitoring and

evaluation and the least positive (or most negative) impact on service delivery.

TABLE 49

Effect of Federal Fiscal Accountability
Requirements on State Programs

| Scale/ Value | Assessment | Number of Responses[a] | | | Number of States[b] | | |
|---|---|---|---|---|---|---|---|
| | | State Administrative Capacity | Service Delivery | SSD Monitoring & Evaluation | State Administrative Capacity | Service Delivery | SSD Monitoring & Evaluation |
| 1 | Strongly Negative | 11 | 19 | 8 | 1 | 2 | 1 |
| 2 | Negative | 13 | 14 | 6 | 5 | 13 | 3 |
| 3 | No Impact | 13 | 12 | 16 | 16 | 18 | 12 |
| 4 | Positive | 8 | 6 | 6 | 24 | 16 | 32 |
| 5 | Strongly Positive | 2 | -- | 2 | 4 | 2 | 3 |
| -- | No Response | -- | -- | -- | 1 | -- | -- |
| | Total | 47 | 51 | 38 | 51 | 51 | 51 |
| | Mean Response | 2.5 | 2.1 | 2.7 | 3.5 | 3.0 | 3.6 |

a. The Urban Institute Title XX Study: 8 State In-Depth Study.
b. The Urban Institute Title XX Study: HEW Regional Office Survey.

E.  **EXTENT OF PREVENTIVE MEASURES TO LIMIT POTENTIAL FOR AUDIT EXCEPTIONS OR FEDERAL FISCAL SANCTIONS**

Respondents in the eight-state study and observers in the federal regional offices were asked the following question:

> To what extent does this state take preventive measures to limit the potential for audit exceptions or federal fiscal sanctions?

The responses of regional office and state personnel were obtained on a scale from 1 (indicating not at all) to 5 (indicating a great deal). These data were felt to be important because of the continuing criticism that Title XX has imposed on public and private providers unnecessarily duplicative fiscal management requirements.

Over 80 percent of all responses (at the federal regional office and state levels) indicated that at least moderate steps were taken to limit the potential for audit exceptions or federal fiscal sanctions (see table 50).  Most frequently cited measures taken by states included checking with regional offices (including obtaining written clarification), conduct of fiscal reviews and program monitoring, and special audits of Title XX programs.

As a partial response to the criticism that Title XX was an over-regulated grant-in-aid program (and in order to implement the client employment, group eligibility, and family provisions of P.L. 94-401), HEW promulgated a set of "new freedom" regulations in 1977.  The purpose of these regulations was to eliminate the most criticized aspects of the existing Title XX regulations (e.g., prohibitions against simplified or

TABLE 50

Extent to Which States Take Preventive Measures
to Limit Potential for Audit Exceptions
or Federal Fiscal Sanctions

| Scale/<br>Value | Response | 8-State Responses | | Regional Office<br>Instruments | |
|---|---|---|---|---|---|
| | | No. of<br>Responses | Percent<br>of Total | No. of<br>States | Percent<br>of Total |
| 1 | Not at All | 3 | 4.7 | 1 | 2.0 |
| 2 | Less than Moderate | 8 | 12.5 | 7 | 13.7 |
| 3 | Moderate | 19 | 29.7 | 13 | 25.5 |
| 4 | More than Moderate | 22 | 34.4 | 17 | 33.3 |
| 5 | A Great Deal | 12 | 18.7 | 13 | 25.5 |
| | Total | 64 | 100.0 | 51 | 100.0 |
| | AVERAGE ASSESSMENT | | 3.5 | | 3.7 |

"declaration" forms of client eligibility determination, requirements

for individual basic data files under SSRR, restrictive definitions

of what could be considered a "protective service," and prohibitions

against institutional and subsistence programs even in cases where they

constituted an "integral and subordinate" feature of a Title XX social

service), thereby granting to states "new freedom" in the design of their

social services programs.

F.   CONCLUSION

1. There appears to be consensus about what the federal role under
Title XX is NOT, but little clarity about what that role should be.

It is apparent that the federal government played a much stronger

role in setting priorities for social services prior to Title XX.  A 1973

Urban Institute study suggested, in fact, that the role of federal actors

in the decision-making process often exceeded their authority.  The strength

of the federal role stemmed partly from actual statutory authority granted

to the federal government under Titles IV-A and VI (the predecessor legis-

lation to Title XX) and partly from a tradition of direct interaction between

federal program (i.e., social services) personnel and their counterpart pro-

fessionals at the state level.  This direct interaction between professionals,

bypassing elected officials, has been described as "picket-fence" federalism.

In the era of "New Federalism," from which Title XX emerged, greater

reliance was to be placed on the elected officials of general-purpose govern-

ment.  In the case of social services, this meant that governors, for example, were given a lead responsibility in the formulation and approval of the CASP plan. That decisions about what social services are to be provided to which people (within statutory bounds) are to be made at the state level appears to have been accepted by federal officials. Regional office personnel consistently acknowledge that it is beyond the scope of their authority to direct state decisions in this regard.

What does not appear to have emerged, however, are clear pictures of what Title XX is expected to accomplish and what the appropriate federal role in social services should be. Without answers to such fundamental questions, it has been impossible, for example, to delineate the respective responsibilities of the central and regional offices of the Administration for Public Services.

2. There exists an opportunity for a more positive federal role in the implementation of Title XX.

This paper is not an appropriate forum for defining a more positive role for the federal government in social services. The Institute's evaluation of Title XX's implementation has generally attempted to be descriptive rather than prescriptive. Nevertheless, the following brief discussion of some of the elements which the authors believe would enhance the federal role may prove helpful to the reader.

a. More Relevant Technical Assistance. Much of the "assistance" provided by HEW to state Title XX agencies is not assistance at all. As suggested earlier (see table 47), the most typical form of regional office support to state agencies is policy interpretation.

Although policy interpretation was rated by state respondents as the most useful form of support provided by regional offices, this was most often observed to be grounded in protection and tradition and conditioned upon the presumed expertise of regional office staff. SSDs often were observed attempting to secure the a priori assurance of HEW that a particular course of action was, in fact, permitted under federal statute and regulations. This traditional pattern of intergovernmental relations is, perhaps, an unnecessary legacy from the period of conflict and audit exceptions that preceded Title XX's implementation. Most of the rhetoric, at least, surrounding Title XX suggests that a new pattern of intergovernmental relations is in order.

The principal areas in which more relevant technical assistance could be offered by regional and central office staff (given adequate training) in lieu of policy interpretation are program evaluation, service reporting, and interagency coordination. This latter area (program coordination) is particularly appropriate to Title XX, since state and local agencies are typically faced with the challenge of integrating a variety of human resource programs into a single service delivery system. Each of the programs typically provided by an SSD (e.g., social services, child welfare services, Medicaid, public assistance, and food stamps) is administered by separate divisions of the federal Office of Human Development Services, different arms of HEW, or the Department of Agriculture. This suggests both the opportunity and need for more cross-program technical assistance.

b.  <u>More Balanced Federal Assistance and Monitoring</u>.  As previously
noted, the bulk of the nation's social services programs are administered
by agencies other than the SSD.  Nevertheless, it was the authors' obser-
vation that state social services agencies received the bulk of federal
technical assistance provided under Title XX.  Federal audits often stop
at the point of reviewing state contracts with providers of purchased
services.  As a result, the delivery of the bulk of the state's social
service program may not be monitored.

Governors, state legislatures, budget officers, and their staffs were
often observed to play key roles in the resource allocation and social
services priority-setting process.  Yet HEW assistance to these offices
has been uneven and discontinuous.

c. <u>Leadership in Evaluation</u>.  Perhaps the clearest role for the federal
government set forth in Title XX is evaluation.  One of the arguments in favor
of Title XX-type legislation was that it would enable the federal government
to focus on the extent to which diverse state service initiatives were or
were not accomplishing their goals.

A component of a more positive federal role, then, could be the development of a reasonably durable framework for social services evaluation by HEW
and state social services agencies.  It may not be too late, for example,
to make the national goals of Title XX (e.g., self-support and self-
sufficiency) more useful as criteria against which state service performance
may be assessed.

Given the diversity of state and local programs, too, the opportunity exists for the more extensive use of natural experiments. The results of such experiments may, over time, contribute to the national understanding of what works in social services.

c. Network Management. An opportunity for positive federal leadership in social services also exists in network management. It is clearly accepted by all parties, as noted above, that the federal government does not, for the most part, direct state and local social services programs. The responsibility for social services administration, which is subject only to rather broad federal guidelines, rests heavily with state social services agencies.

In spite of the diversity of state programs, however, the authors have observed that many states share the same problems (e.g., separation, inter-title transfers, compliance with the 50-percent rule, substate allocation, purchase of service monitoring, and SSRR utilization). Only through the most informal means can a state learn whether other states are facing problems similar to its own. Although national professional organizations and research and consulting institutions can, and do, fill some of this information void, there is room for positive federal leadership in facilitating interaction among, and lending expertise to, states with common interests and concerns.

d. Effecting Accountability. The final component of the more positive federal role in Title XX administration suggested by the authors is in effecting or perfecting the means of state-level accountability. As indicated repeatedly, Title XX assumes that state social services programs will be accountable primarily to the people of each state. The primary instrument of state-level accountability under Title XX is the Comprehensive Annual Services Program (CASP) plan. Other, perhaps more traditional, means of accountability (e.g., state budget processes, client participation, advisory groups, and legislative oversight) are unevenly utilized by the states.

It seems legitimate for HEW, as the statutory guardian of the Title XX process, to advocate and otherwise act to assure more meaningful CASP planning, more extensive integration of planning with budgeting, cooperation with legislative reviews of social services programs, and more meaningful participation on the part of both consumers of social services and the general public.